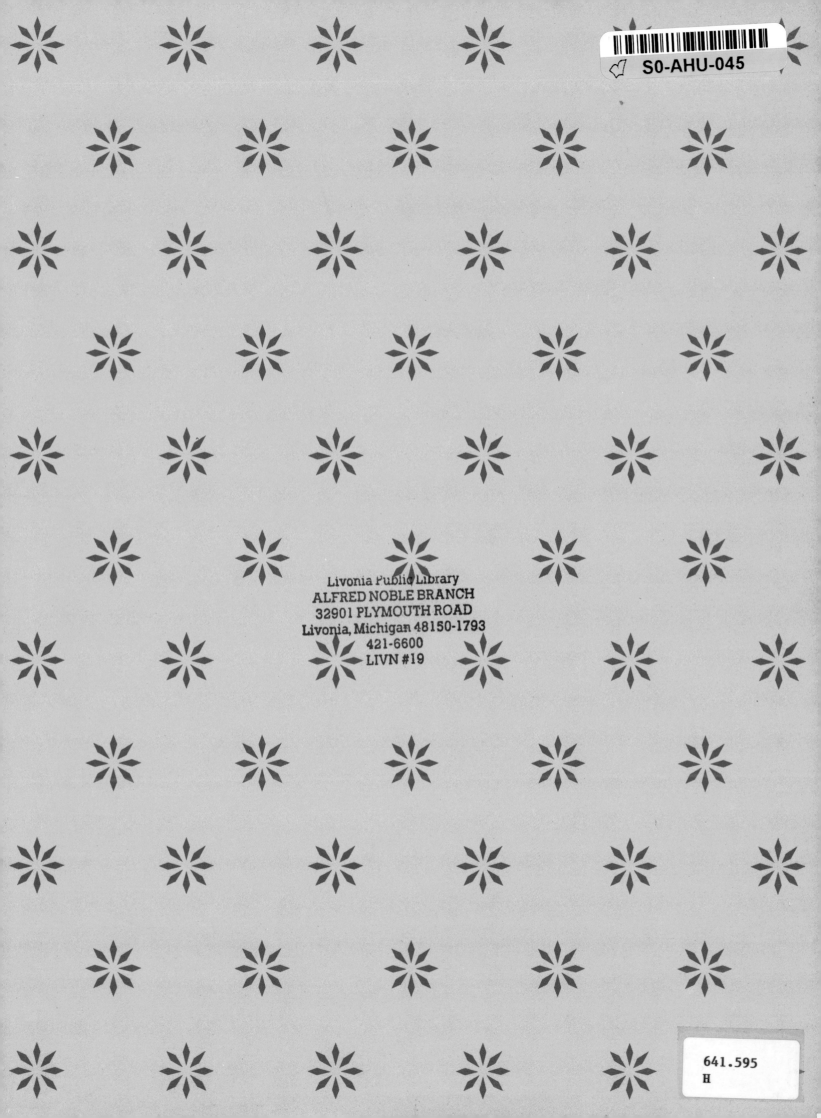

THE COMPLETE
❖ BOOK OF ❖
INDIAN
COOKING

THE COMPLETE

❖ BOOK OF ❖

INDIAN COOKING

The ultimate Indian cookery collection,
with over 170 delicious and authentic recipes

SHEHZAD HUSAIN AND
RAFI FERNANDEZ

LORENZ BOOKS

This edition published by Lorenz Books
27 West 20th Street, New York, NY 10011;

LORENZ BOOKS are available for bulk purchase for sales promotion and for premium use. For details, write or call the sales director, Lorenz Books, 27 West 20th street, New York, NY 10011; (800) 354-9657

Lorenz Books is an imprint of
Anness Publishing Inc.
Anness Publishing Limited
Hermes House
88-89 Blackfriars Road
London SE1 8HA

MAY 16 2000

ISBN 0-7548-0175-6

Publisher: Joanna Lorenz   3 9082 07819 5420
Project Editors: Judith Simons, Lindsay Porter
Designers: David Rowley, Ian Sandom
Jacket Designer: Nigel Partridge
Photographers: David Armstrong, Edward Allwright
Home Economists: Shehzad Husain, Stephen Wheeler
Nutritional Data: Wendy Doyle

Jacket photograph of Shehzad Husain © Tony Isbitt Indian Fruit
Salad recipe (page 230) by Stephen Wheeler

Printed and bound in Singapore

© Anness Publishing limited 1995
Updated © 1999
10 9 8 7 6 5 4 3 2 1

MEASUREMENTS

Three sets of equivalent measurements have been provided in the recipes here, in the following order: Metric, Imperial and American. It is essential that units of measurements are not mixed within each recipe. Where conversions result in awkward numbers, these have been rounded for convenience, but are accurate enough to produce successful results.

NOTE

The nutritional analyses accompanying the Low Fat Option recipes were prepared using a computer program called FOODBASE which is based on data from McCance & Widdowson's The Composition of Foods, with fatty acid data from The Institute of Brain Chemistry and Human Nutrition. Ingredients specified as optional have not been included in the related analysis and, where weights have not been given in the recipes, an approximate value has been calculated.

Contents

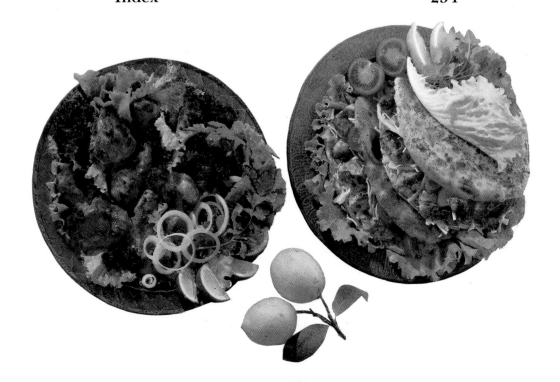

Introduction

THE vast sub-continent of India offers a range of culinary delights as rich and diverse as its people and history. Each region has its own unique cooking style: cream, yogurt, ghee and nuts feature in dishes in the north, while the south favours chillies, coconut and coconut oil. Fish and mustard oil predominate in the east while the west has incorporated the greatest number of foreign ingredients. One element unites these diverse styles – the use of spices to create the flavours and aromas distinctive of Indian cuisine.

The flavours of Indian food are appreciated all over the world and although delicious, the nutritional content of some traditional Indian dishes has been at odds with our modern view of healthy eating. Liberal use of ghee, which is clarified butter, adds an unwelcome quantity of saturated fat to Indian dishes.

In Western society, the healthy eating message is clear. Eat less fat, in particular saturated fat, less sugar and salt and more fibre. This means stepping up our intake of complex carbohydrates, fruit and vegetables and eating more fish and leaner meats. However, healthy ingredients such as fresh vegetables, lentils and pulses, and seafood are widely used in Indian cuisine. Poultry is usually cooked without the skin which is where most of the fat resides and good Indian cooks will always use lean meat or meat trimmed of excess fat. So if you want to reduce your fat intake, there is no need to forego tasty Indian food. Among the recipes in this book, you will find a selection of low-fat recipes, which have been carefully designed to give an optimum nutritional profile without sacrificing flavour.

Balti cooking is a fairly new experience in the West, but the craze has spread like wildfire, with Balti restaurants springing up overnight and becoming instantly popular. The essence of Balti cuisine is the speed of cooking – it's almost as fast as Chinese stir-frying. The equipment needed is a wok shaped pan, known as a "karahi". The type of food cooked in the karahi is eclectic, drawing its influences from many different countries such as Iran and Afghanistan, and now the West is contributing its own style.

When made at home, Balti cooking is fast, fun and simply delicious. Once you have tried the basic recipes, make up your own dishes using different combinations of ingredients.

Although the original karahi was made of cast iron, modern varieties come in a selection of metals. The essential quality is that they must be sturdy enough to withstand high cooking temperatures and sizzling oils. They are fun to use but it is not absolutely essential to use the authentic Balti pan; a fairly thick Chinese wok or deep round-based frying pan are good substitutes. Balti pans also come in small sizes for individual servings complete with wooden stands so that you can bring them to the table for serving.

Below left and below: *Beef with green beans and Balti baby vegetables provide traditional flavours without sacrificing today's requirements for healthy eating.*

Cooking Equipment

You should find that your own kitchen is well equipped with everything you need to produce the dishes in this book. Good-quality saucepans with heavy bases, and wooden spoons and a slotted spoon to use with them, mixing bowls, sharp knives, a chopping board, a sieve (strainer) and a rolling pin are the main essentials. A balloon whisk for beating yogurt and a pastry brush for basting kebabs (kabobs) with marinade may also be useful for some of the recipes.

A heavy-based frying pan (skillet) is a must, and you may like to try cooking some of the dishes in a traditional Indi-an karahi or Balti pan – a deep, round-bottomed vessel with two circular carrying handles. Karahis are very sturdy and therefore capable of withstanding high cooking temperatures and sizzling oils. Wooden stands are available, too, so the pans can be brought to the table to serve. The other specialist cooking vessel used in the Indian kitchen is a tava, a flat cast-iron frying pan used for cooking chapatis and other breads and for roasting spices, but any sturdy frying pan can be substituted.

A food processor or blender is a great labour-saving tool and will be invalu-able for making pastes or puréeing ing-redients. Whole spices can be freshly ground using a mortar and pestle, or, if you have one, a coffee grinder makes the job so much easier.

Cooking Equipment

1 *food processor* **2** *mortar and pestle* **3** *Balti pan, or karahi, for serving individual portions* **4** *medium mixing bowl* **5** *good quality, heavy-based saucepans in two sizes* **6** *well-seasoned traditional Balti pan, or karahi* **7** *coffee grinder* **8** *deep, round-bottomed frying pan (skillet)* **9** *large mixing bowl* **10** *sieve (strainer)* **11** *sharp knives in three sizes* **12** *slotted spoon* **13** *wooden spoons* **14** *rolling pin*

Making Ginger and Garlic Pulp

Ginger and garlic pulp is specified in many of the recipes here and it can be time-consuming to peel and process these every time. It's much easier to make the pulps in large quantities and use as needed. The method is the same for both ingredients. The pulp can be stored in an airtight container or jar in the refrigerator for four to six weeks. Alternatively, freeze in ice-cube trays kept for the purpose (the pulps will taint the trays slightly). Add 1 tsp of the pulp to each compartment, freeze, remove from the tray and store in the freezer in a plastic bag.

1 Take about 225 g/8 oz fresh ginger or garlic and soak overnight – this softens the skins and makes them easy to peel. Peel and place in a food processor or blender.

2 Process until pulped, adding a little water to get the right consistency, if necessary.

Home-Made Garam Masala

Garam masala can be purchased ready-ground in various mixtures. For an ultra-fresh, home-made variety, try this combination of spices.

4 × 2.5 cm/1 in cinnamon sticks
3 cloves
3 black peppercorns
2 black cardamom pods, with husks removed
2 tsp black cumin seeds

Grind the spices together in a coffee grinder or using a mortar and pestle until quite fine and use in any recipe calling for garam masala.

A Question of Taste

The spices used in a dish are integral to its flavour. One spice can completely alter the taste of a dish and a combination of several will also affect its colour and texture. The quantities of spices and salt specified in this book are merely a guide, so feel free to experiment.

This is particularly true of chilli powder and fresh and dried chillies; some brands and varieties are hotter than others. Experiment with quantities, adding less than specified, if wished. Much of the fiery heat of fresh chillies is contained in the seeds, and these can be removed by splitting the chillies down the middle and washing them away under cold running water. You can also remove the seeds from dried chillies. Wash your hands thoroughly with soap and water after handling cut chillies and avoid touching your face – particularly your lips and eyes – for a good while afterwards.

Cooking Tips

• The final colour and texture of a curry depend on how well you brown the onions in the first stage of cooking. Heat the oil first, add the onions, then reduce the heat slightly. Stir the onions only occasionally; excessive stirring will draw the moisture from them which will inhibit the browning process.

• Natural (plain) yogurt produces a wonderful creamy texture and is used in many of the recipes as a healthy alternative to cream. Always beat the yogurt with a fork first and then add it to the pan gradually, stirring continuously, to prevent it curdling.

• Some recipes specify whole spices, such as cinnamon sticks, cardamom pods and cloves. If wished, remove these from the dish before serving.

• There is no substitute for fresh coriander (cilantro) and the more used the better as it imparts a beautiful aroma and flavour. Happily, coriander is now readily available from most supermarkets, and more economically from Asian stores. If wished, buy a large quantity and freeze whatever you don't need. Simply cut off the roots and any thick stalks, wash the leaves in cold water and leave to drain in a sieve (strainer). When dry, chop and store in plastic bags or airtight containers in the freezer. Do not defrost before using.

Below: Spices are used both whole and ground in Indian cooking. If possible, buy whole spices and grind them at home for a more pungent aroma and intense flavour.

Choosing Ingredients

Good food, whatever the cuisine, depends on the quality of the ingredients used – as well as the skill of the cook. In India a wonderful array of fresh vegetables, fruit, herbs and spices, as well as dried spices, can be found in the numerous markets and street stalls, and a choice of the best available is often purchased on a daily basis. Nowadays, a good range of fruit, herbs and vegetables, including exotic items, can now be found in supermarkets or can be purchased from specialist Asian stores. Take advantage of the fresh produce available to produce these delicious dishes, and don't be afraid to substitute other fresh vegetables if a specified ingredient can't be found.

Meat and poultry purchased from a good butcher is best, and if you are a regular customer they will usually pre-prepare the cuts you want, trimming, skinning and boning the meat as necessary. Fresh seafood and fish is always preferable to frozen; however, frozen foods are undoubtedly a boon for the busy cook and for quick weekday meals.

The more common spices can be found in supermarkets, and the others can be purchased from Asian stores. Some spices are available ready-ground and they keep well if stored in airtight containers. In Pakistan and India we almost always buy whole spices and grind them ourselves just prior to cooking: for a special meal the flavour can't be beaten and if you have a coffee grinder it's quite quick to do.

Below: Good quality ingredients are the basis of successful cooking. Choose fruits and vegetables at their peak for best results, and ensure dry ingredients have not been stored too long for maximum flavour.

Glossary of Special Ingredients

Almonds Blanched almonds are available whole, flaked (slivered) and ground, and impart a sumptuous richness to curries. They are considered a great delicacy in India, where they are extremely expensive.

Aniseed This has a delicate liquorice flavour and sweet seeds. It is a good aid to digestion.

Asafoetida This is a resin with an acrid and bitter taste and a strong odour. Store in a jar with a strong airtight seal to prevent the smell dispersing into other ingredients.

Basmati rice If possible, try to use basmati rice for all savoury rice dishes – the delicate flavour is unbeatable.

Bay leaves The large dried leaves of the bay laurel tree are one of the oldest herbs used in cookery.

Bengal gram Bengal gram is used whole in lentil curries. The flour (besan) is used to prepare bhajias and may be used to flavour and thicken curries.

Black-eyed peas These white kidney-shaped beans with a black "eye" are available dried or canned.

Cardamom pods This spice is native to India, where it is considered to be the most prized spice after saffron. The pods can be used whole or the husks can be removed to release the seeds, and they have a slightly pungent but very aromatic taste. They come in three varieties: green, white and black. The green and white pods can be used for both sweet and savoury dishes or to flavour rice. The black pods are used only for savoury dishes.

Cashew nuts These full-flavoured nuts are a popular ingredient in many kinds of Asian cooking.

Chana dhal This is a round split yellow lentil, similar in appearance to the smaller moong dhal and the larger yellow split pea, which can be used as a substitute. It is used as a binding agent in some dishes and is widely available from Asian stores.

Chapati (ata) flour This is a type of wholemeal (whole-wheat) flour available from Asian stores and is used to make chapatis and other breads. Ordinary wholemeal flour can be used as a substitute if well sifted.

Chick-peas (garbanzos) This nutty tasting pulse is widely used in Indian vegetarian dishes.

Chillies – dried red These hot peppers are extremely fiery and should be used with caution. The heat can be toned down by removing the seeds before use. Dried chillies can be used whole or coarsely crushed.

Chillies – fresh Green chillies are not indigenous to India but have become indispensable to Indian cuisine. They are very rich in vitamins A and C.

Chilli powder Also known as cayenne pepper, this fiery ground spice should be used with caution. The heat can vary from brand to brand, so adjust quantities to suit your tastebuds.

Cinnamon One of the earliest known spices, cinnamon has an aromatic and sweet flavour. It is sold ready-ground and as sticks.

Cloves This spice is used to flavour many sweet and savoury dishes and is usually added whole.

Coconut Used to flavour both sweet and savoury dishes, fresh coconut is now frequently available from supermarkets. Desiccated (shredded) coconut and creamed coconut make acceptable substitutes for most dishes.

Coriander – fresh (cilantro) This beautifully fragrant herb is used both in cooking and sprinkled over dishes as an attractive garnish.

Coriander seeds This aromatic spice has a pungent, slightly lemony flavour. The seeds are used widely, either coarsely ground or in powdered form, in meat, fish and poultry dishes. Ground coriander, a brownish powder, is an important constituent of any mixture of curry spices.

Cumin "White" cumin seeds are oval, ridged and greenish brown in colour. They have a strong aroma and flavour and can be used whole or ground. Ready-ground cumin powder is widely available. Black cumin seeds are dark and aromatic and are used to flavour curries and rice.

Curry leaves Similar in appearance to bay leaves but with a very different flavour, these can be bought dried and occasionally fresh from Asian stores. Fresh leaves freeze well.

Fennel seeds Very similar in appearance to cumin seeds, fennel seeds have a very sweet taste and are used to flavour certain curries. They can also be chewed as a mouth-freshener after a spicy meal.

Fenugreek – fresh Sold in bunches, this herb has very small leaves and is used to flavour meat and vegetarian dishes. Always discard the stalks, which will impart a bitterness to a dish if used.

Fenugreek seeds These flat seeds are extremely pungent and slightly bitter.

Five-spice powder This is a combination of star anise, fennel, cinnamon, clove and Sichuan pepper.

Garam masala This is a mixture of spices which can be made from freshly ground spices at home or purchased ready-made. There is no set recipe, but a typical mixture might include black cumin seeds, peppercorns, cloves, cinnamon and black cardamon pods.

Garlic This is a standard ingredient, along with ginger, in most curries. It can be used pulped, crushed or chopped. Whole cloves are sometimes added to dishes.

Ghee This is clarified butter and was once the main cooking fat used in Indian cooking. Nowadays, vegetable ghee or vegetable oil – particularly corn oil – are used in its place, being lower in saturated fat.

Ginger One of the most popular spices in India and also one of the oldest, fresh ginger is an important ingredient in many curries and is now widely available. Dried powdered ginger is a useful standby.

Mace Mace is the dried covering of the nutmeg. It has a slightly bitter taste.

Mangoes Ripe fresh mangoes are used in sweet dishes, while green or unripe mangoes are sometimes used in curries and to make mango chutney.

Mango powder Made from dried unripe mangoes, this has a sour taste.

Masoor dhal These split red lentils are actually orange in colour and turn a pale yellow when cooked. Whole brown lentils are a type of red lentil with the husk intact.

Mint Indian mint has a stronger aroma than the varieties available in the West.

Moong dhal This teardrop-shaped split yellow lentil is similar to, though smaller than, chana dhal.

Mustard seeds – black Round in shape and sharp in flavour, black mustard seeds are used for flavouring curries and pickles.

Nigella Nigella is an aromatic spice with a sharp and tingling taste. It is mainly used in vegetable dishes.

Nutmeg Although not widely used in Indian cooking, nutmeg is sometimes used either freshly grated or ready-ground to add a sweet flavour.

Onion seeds Black in colour and triangular in shape, these seeds are widely used in pickles and to flavour vegetable curries.

Paneer This is a white, smooth-textured cheese, available from Asian stores. It is excellent used in combination with meat and fish or as a vegetarian replacement and it appears in several of the dishes in this book. Long-life vacuum-packed paneer is available from Indian stores and some health-food shops. (See Paneer Balti with Prawns/Shrimp for a simple recipe for home-made paneer.)

Peppercorns Black peppercorns are sometimes used whole with other whole spices, such as cloves, cardamon pods and bay leaves, to flavour curries. Otherwise, whenever possible, use freshly ground or crushed black pepper if the recipe calls for it.

Pistachios These sweet, green nuts are not indigenous to India and are therefore an expensive ingredient.

Pomegranate seeds These can be extracted from fresh pomegranates or bought in jars from Asian stores and impart a delicious tangy flavour.

Poppy seeds These seeds are usually used toasted to bring out the flavour.

Red gram Red gram is available dry or lightly oiled.

Saffron The world's most expensive spice is the dried stigmas of the saffron crocus, which is native to Asia Minor. It takes 250,000 flowers to make just 450 g/1 lb saffron. Fortunately, only a small quantity of saffron is needed to flavour and colour a dish, whether sweet or savoury. Saffron is sold as strands and in powder form, and has a beautiful flavour and aroma.

Sesame seeds These seeds have a slightly nutty taste.

Star anise Star anise is a star-shaped, liquorice-flavoured pod.

Tamarind The dried black pods of the tamarind plant are sour in taste and very sticky. Tamarind can now be bought in paste form in jars, although lemon juice can be used as a substitute.

Toor dhal A shiny split lentil, toor dhal is similar in size to chana dhal.

Turmeric This bright yellow, bitter-tasting spice is sold ground. It is used mainly for colour rather than flavour.

Urid dhal (black gram) Also known as black gram, this lentil is similar in size to moong dhal and is available either with the blackish hull retained or removed. Inside, the lentil is a creamy white. It takes a long time to cook and has a slightly drier texture than moong dhal.

Vermicelli These hair-like strands are made from wheat and are used in savoury and sweet dishes.

Walnuts Walnuts are used in sweetmeats, salads and raitas.

Below: *A well-stocked store cupboard might include lentils, pulses and seeds and dried herbs and spices. Buy in quantities you know you will be able to use, as some ingredients lose their potency over time.*

Appetizers & Snacks

Spicy pastries such as Vegetable Samosas and crisp Onion Bhajias are familiar starters. However, you'll find a whole host of other tempting dishes here as well. Try spicy Grilled Prawns as a first course, or go for the tasty low-fat version of Chicken Tikka. There are soups, too, some fairly fiery and others which are more subtly spiced.

Onion Bhajias

Bhajias are a classic snack of India. The same batter may be used with a variety of vegetables.

MAKES 20–25

INGREDIENTS
225 g/8 oz/2 cups gram flour (besan)
1/2 tsp chilli powder
1 tsp turmeric
1 tsp baking powder
1/4 tsp asafoetida
salt, to taste
1/2 tsp each, nigella, fennel, cumin and onion seeds, coarsely crushed
2 large onions, finely sliced
2 green chillies, finely chopped
50 g/2 oz/2 cups fresh coriander (cilantro), chopped
cold water, to mix
vegetable oil, for deep-frying

1 ▲ In a bowl, mix together the flour, chilli, turmeric, baking powder, asafoetida and salt to taste. Pass through a sieve (strainer) into a large mixing bowl.

2 Add the coarsely crushed seeds, onion, green chillies and fresh coriander (cilantro) and toss together well. Very gradually mix in enough cold water to make a thick batter surrounding all the ingredients.

3 ▲ Heat enough oil in a karahi or wok for deep-frying. Drop spoonfuls of the mixture into the hot oil and fry until they are golden brown. Leave enough space to turn the bhajias. Drain well and serve hot.

Yogurt Soup

Some communities in India add sugar to this soup. When Bhajias are added, it is served as a main dish.

SERVES 4–6

INGREDIENTS
450 ml/3/4 pint/scant 2 cups natural (plain) yogurt, beaten
4 tbsp gram flour (besan)
1/2 tsp chilli powder
1/2 tsp ground turmeric
salt, to taste
2–3 fresh green chillies, finely chopped
4 tbsp vegetable oil
4 dried red chillies
1 tsp cumin seeds
3 cloves garlic, crushed
1 piece fresh ginger, 5 cm/2 in long, crushed

3–4 curry leaves
1 tbsp chopped fresh coriander (cilantro)

2 ▲ Heat the oil in a frying pan (skillet) and fry the remaining spices, garlic and ginger until the dried chillies turn black. Add the curry leaves and fresh coriander (cilantro) to the pan.

1 ▲ Mix together the first 5 ingredients and pass through a strainer into a saucepan. Add the green chillies and cook gently for about 10 minutes, stirring occasionally. Be careful not to let the soup boil over.

3 Pour most of the oil and the spices over the yogurt soup, cover the pan and leave to rest for 5 minutes off the heat. Mix well and gently reheat for a further 5 minutes. Serve hot, garnished with the remaining oil and spices.

Onion Bhajias (top) and Yogurt Soup

Spicy Chicken and Mushroom Soup

This creamy chicken soup makes a hearty meal for a winter's night. Serve it piping hot with fresh garlic bread.

SERVES 4

INGREDIENTS

225 g/8 oz chicken, skinned and boned
75 g/3 oz/6 tbsp unsalted butter
1/2 tsp garlic pulp
1 tsp garam masala
1 tsp crushed black peppercorns
1 tsp salt
1/4 tsp ground nutmeg
1 medium leek, sliced
75 g/3 oz/1 cup mushrooms, sliced
50 g/2 oz/1/3 cup sweetcorn (corn kernels)
300 ml/1/2 pint/1 1/4 cups water
250 ml/8 fl oz/1 cup single (light) cream
1 tbsp chopped fresh coriander (cilantro)
1 tsp crushed dried red chillies (optional)

1 Cut the chicken pieces into very fine strips.

2 ▲ Melt the butter in a medium saucepan. Lower the heat slightly and add the garlic and garam masala. Lower the heat even further and add the black peppercorns, salt and nutmeg. Finally, add the chicken pieces, leek, mushrooms and sweetcorn (corn kernels), and cook for 5–7 minutes or until the chicken is cooked through, stirring constantly.

3 ▲ Remove from the heat and allow to cool slightly. Transfer three-quarters of the mixture into a food processor or blender. Add the water and process for about 1 minute.

4 Pour the resulting purée back into the saucepan with the rest of the mixture and bring to the boil over a medium heat. Lower the heat and stir in the cream.

5 ▲ Add the fresh coriander (cilantro) and taste for seasoning. Serve hot, garnished with the crushed red chillies, if wished.

Chicken and Almond Soup

This soup makes an excellent appetizer and served with Naan will also make a satisfying lunch or supper dish.

SERVES 4

INGREDIENTS

75 g/3 oz/6 tbsp unsalted butter
1 medium leek, chopped
1/2 tsp shredded ginger
75 g/3 oz/1 cup ground almonds
1 tsp salt
1/2 tsp crushed black peppercorns
1 fresh green chilli, chopped
1 medium carrot, sliced
50 g/2 oz/1/2 cup frozen peas
115g/4 oz/3/4 cup chicken, skinned, boned
    and cubed
1 tbsp chopped fresh coriander (cilantro)
450 ml/3/4 pint/scant 2 cups water
250 ml/8 fl oz/1 cup single (light) cream
4 coriander sprigs

1 Melt the butter in a large karahi or deep round-bottomed frying pan (skillet), and sauté the leek with the ginger until soft.

2 ▲ Lower the heat and add the ground almonds, salt, peppercorns, chilli, carrot, peas and chicken. Fry for about 10 minutes or until the chicken is completely cooked, stirring constantly. Add the chopped fresh coriander (cilantro).

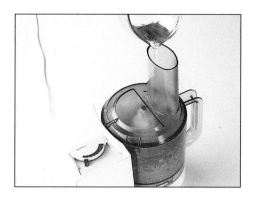

3 ▲ Remove from the heat and allow to cool slightly. Transfer the mixture to a food processor or blender and process for about 1½ minutes. Pour in the water and blend for a further 30 seconds.

4 ▲ Pour back into the saucepan and bring to the boil, stirring occasionally. Once it has boiled, lower the heat and gradually stir in the cream. Cook gently for a further 2 minutes, stirring occasionally.

5 Serve garnished with the fresh coriander sprigs.

South Indian Pepper Water

This is a highly soothing broth for winter evenings, also known as Mulla-ga-tani. Serve with the whole spices or strain and reheat if you so wish. The lemon juice may be adjusted to taste, but this dish should be distinctly sour.

SERVES 4–6

INGREDIENTS
2 tbsp vegetable oil
1/2 tsp freshly ground black pepper
1 tsp cumin seeds
1/2 tsp mustard seeds
1/4 tsp asafoetida
2 dried red chillies
4–6 curry leaves
1/2 tsp turmeric
2 cloves garlic, crushed
300 ml/1/2 pint/1 1/4 cups tomato juice
juice of 2 lemons

120 ml/4 fl oz/1/2 cup water
salt, to taste
fresh coriander (cilantro), chopped, to
    garnish (optional)

2 ▲ Lower the heat and add the tomato juice, lemon juice, water and salt. Bring to the boil then simmer for 10 minutes. Garnish with the chopped coriander (cilantro), if wished, and serve.

1 ▲ In a large pan, heat the oil and fry the next 8 ingredients until the chillies are nearly black and the garlic golden brown.

Chicken Mulligatawny

Using the original Pepper Water – Mulla-ga-tani – this dish was created by the non-vegetarian chefs during the British Raj. The recipe was imported to the West and today features on many restaurant menus where it is often called simply Mulligatawny Soup.

SERVES 4–6

INGREDIENTS
900 g/2 lb/6 1/2 cups chicken, skinned,
    boned and cubed
600 ml/1 pint/2 1/2 cups water
6 green cardamom pods
1 piece cinnamon stick, 5 cm/2 in long
4–6 curry leaves
1 tbsp ground coriander
1 tsp ground cumin
1/2 tsp turmeric
3 cloves garlic, crushed
12 whole peppercorns
4 cloves

1 onion, finely chopped
115 g/4 oz creamed coconut
salt, to taste
juice of 2 lemons
deep-fried onions, to garnish

2 ▲ Reheat the stock in the pan. Add all the remaining ingredients, except the chicken and deep-fried onions. Simmer for 10–15 minutes, then strain and return the chicken to the soup. Reheat the soup and serve garnished with the deep-fried onions.

1 ▲ Place the chicken in a large pan with the water and cook until the chicken is tender. Skim the surface, then remove the chicken with a slotted spoon and keep warm.

South Indian Pepper Water (top) and Chicken Mulligatawny

Tomato and Coriander (Cilantro) Soup

LOW-FAT RECIPE

Although soups are not often eaten in India or Pakistan, tomato soup seems to be among the most popular ones. It is excellent on a cold winter's day.

SERVES 4

INGREDIENTS
675 g/1½ lb tomatoes
2 tbsp vegetable oil
1 bay leaf
4 spring onions (scallions), chopped
1 tsp salt
½ tsp garlic pulp
1 tsp crushed black peppercorns
2 tbsp chopped fresh coriander (cilantro)
750 ml/1¼ pints/good 3 cups water
1 tbsp cornflour (cornstarch)

Garnish
1 spring onion (scallion), chopped (optional)
2 tbsp single (light) cream (optional)

NUTRITIONAL VALUES (per portion)	
Total fat	7.16 g
Saturated fat	1.37 g
Cholesterol	2.80 mg
Energy (kcals/kj)	113/474

1 ▲ To skin the tomatoes, plunge them in very hot water, then take them out more or less straight away. The skin should now peel off quickly and easily. Once this is done chop the tomatoes.

2 ▲ In a medium saucepan, heat the oil and fry the chopped tomatoes, bay leaf and chopped spring onions (scallions) for a few minutes until soft.

3 ▲ Gradually add the salt, garlic, peppercorns and fresh coriander (cilantro) to the tomato mixture, finally adding the water. Bring to the boil, lower the heat and simmer for 15–20 minutes.

4 Dissolve the cornflour (cornstarch) in a little water.

5 ▲ Remove the soup from the heat and press through a sieve (strainer).

6 ▲ Return to the pan, add the cornflour and stir over a gentle heat for about 3 minutes until thickened.

7 Pour into individual serving dishes and garnish with the chopped spring onion and cream, if using. Serve hot with bread.

COOK'S TIP

If the only fresh tomatoes available are rather pale and under-ripe, add 1 tbsp tomato purée (paste) to the pan with the chopped tomatoes to enhance the colour and flavour of the soup.

Lentil Soup

This is a simple, mildly spiced lentil soup, which is a good accompaniment to heavily spiced meat dishes.

SERVES 4–6

INGREDIENTS

1 tbsp ghee
1 large onion, finely chopped
2 cloves garlic, crushed
1 fresh green chilli, chopped
½ tsp turmeric
75 g/3 oz/⅓ cup split red lentils (masoor dhal)
250 ml/8 fl oz/1 cup water
salt, to taste
400 g/14 oz canned tomatoes, chopped
½ tsp sugar
lemon juice, to taste
200 g/7 oz/1 cup plain boiled rice or 2 potatoes, boiled (optional)
fresh coriander (cilantro), chopped, to garnish (optional)

1 ▲ Heat the ghee in a large saucepan and fry the onion, garlic, chilli and turmeric until the onion is translucent.

2 ▲ Add the lentils and water and bring to the boil. Reduce the heat, cover and cook until all the water is absorbed.

3 ▲ Mash the lentils with the back of a wooden spoon until you have a smooth paste. Add salt to taste and mix well.

4 ▲ Add the remaining ingredients and reheat the soup. To provide extra texture, fold in the plain boiled rice or potatoes cut into small cubes. Garnish with coriander (cilantro), if you like, and serve hot.

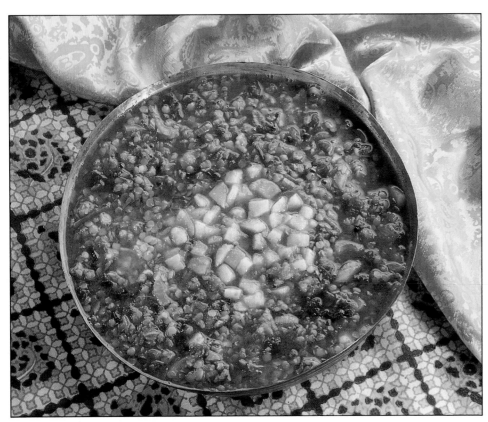

COOK'S TIP

When using lentils, first rinse in cold water and pick over to remove any small stones or loose skins.

Potato Cakes with Stuffing

Only a few communities in India make these unusual potato cakes known as Petis. They can also be served as a main meal with Tomato Salad.

MAKES 8–10

INGREDIENTS
1 tbsp vegetable oil
1 large onion, finely chopped
2 cloves garlic, finely crushed
1 piece fresh ginger, 5 cm/2 in long, finely crushed
1 tsp ground coriander
1 tsp ground cumin
2 fresh green chillies, finely chopped
2 tbsp each, chopped fresh coriander (cilantro) and mint
225 g/8 oz lean minced (ground) beef or lamb
50 g/2 oz/¹/₃ cup frozen peas, thawed
salt, to taste
juice of 1 lemon
900 g/2 lb potatoes, boiled and mashed
2 eggs, beaten
breadcrumbs, for coating
vegetable oil, for shallow-frying
lemon wedges and salad leaves, to serve

1 ▲ Heat the oil and fry the next 7 ingredients until the onion is translucent. Add the meat and peas and fry well until the meat is cooked, then season with salt and lemon juice. The mixture should be very dry.

2 ▲ Divide the mashed potato into 8–10 portions, take one portion at a time and flatten into a pancake in the palm of your hand. Place a spoonful of the meat in the centre and gather the sides together to enclose the meat. Flatten it slightly to make a round.

3 ▲ Dip the cakes in beaten egg and then coat in breadcrumbs. Allow to chill in the refrigerator for about 1 hour.

4 ▲ Heat the oil in a frying pan (skillet) and shallow-fry the cakes until all the sides are brown and crisp. Serve them hot with lemon wedges on a bed of salad leaves.

Chicken Naan Pockets

LOW-FAT RECIPE

This quick-and-easy dish is ideal for a quick snack lunch or supper and excellent as picnic fare. For speed, use the ready-to-bake naans available in some supermarkets and Asian stores, or try warmed pitta bread instead.

SERVES 4

INGREDIENTS
4 naan
3 tbsp natural (plain) low-fat yogurt
1½ tsp garam masala
1 tsp chilli powder
1 tsp salt
3 tbsp lemon juice
1 tbsp chopped fresh coriander (cilantro)
1 fresh green chilli, chopped
450 g/1 lb/3¼ cups chicken, skinned, boned and cubed
1 tbsp vegetable oil (optional)
8 onion rings
2 tomatoes, quartered
½ white cabbage, shredded

Garnish
lemon wedges
2 small tomatoes, halved
mixed salad leaves
fresh coriander (cilantro)

NUTRITIONAL VALUES (per portion)

Total fat	10.85 g
Saturated fat	3.01 g
Cholesterol	65.64 mg
Energy (kcals/kj)	364/1529

1 Cut into the middle of each naan to make a pocket, then set aside.

2 Mix together the yogurt, garam marsala, chilli powder, salt, lemon juice, fresh coriander (cilantro) and chopped green chilli. Pour the marinade over the chicken pieces and leave to marinate for about 1 hour.

3 After 1 hour preheat the grill (broiler) to very hot, then lower the heat to medium. Place the chicken in a flameproof dish and grill (broil) for 15–20 minutes until tender and cooked through, turning the chicken pieces at least twice. If wished, baste with the oil while cooking.

4 ▲ Remove from the heat and fill each naan with the chicken and then with the onion rings, tomatoes and cabbage. Serve with the garnish ingredients.

Chicken Tikka

LOW-FAT RECIPE

This chicken dish is an extremely popular Indian appetizer and is quick and easy to cook. Chicken Tikka can also be served as a main course for four.

SERVES 6

INGREDIENTS
450 g/1 lb/3¼ cups chicken, skinned, boned and cubed
1 tsp ginger pulp
1 tsp garlic pulp
1 tsp chilli powder
¼ tsp turmeric
1 tsp salt
150 ml/¼ pint/⅔ cup natural (plain) low-fat yogurt
4 tbsp lemon juice
1 tbsp chopped fresh coriander (cilantro)
1 tbsp vegetable oil

Garnish
1 small onion, cut into rings
lime wedges
mixed salad
fresh coriander (cilantro)

NUTRITIONAL VALUES (per portion)

Total fat	5.50 g
Saturated fat	1.47 g
Cholesterol	44.07 mg
Energy (kcals/kj)	131/552

1 In a medium bowl, mix together the chicken pieces, ginger, garlic, chilli powder, turmeric, salt, yogurt, lemon juice and fresh coriander (cilantro) and leave to marinate for at least 2 hours.

2 ▲ Place on a grill (broiler) tray or in a flameproof dish lined with foil and baste with the oil.

3 Preheat the grill to medium. Grill (broil) the chicken for 15–20 minutes until cooked, turning and basting 2–3 times. Serve with the garnish ingredients.

Chicken Naan Pockets (top) and Chicken Tikka

Chicken Kofta Balti with Paneer

This rather unusual appetizer looks most elegant when served in small individual karahis.

SERVES 6

INGREDIENTS
Koftas
450 g/1 lb/3¼ cups chicken, skinned, boned and cubed
1 tsp garlic pulp
1 tsp shredded ginger
1½ tsp ground coriander
1½ tsp chilli powder
½ tsp ground fenugreek
¼ tsp turmeric
1 tsp salt
2 tbsp chopped fresh coriander (cilantro)
2 fresh green chillies, chopped
600 ml/1 pint/2½ cups water
corn oil for frying

Paneer mixture
1 medium onion, sliced
1 red (bell) pepper, seeded and cut into strips
1 green (bell) pepper, seeded and cut into strips
175 g/6 oz paneer, cubed
175 g/6 oz/1 cup sweetcorn (corn kernels)

mint sprigs
1 dried red chilli, crushed (optional)

1 ▲ Put all the kofta ingredients, apart from the oil, into a medium saucepan. Bring to the boil slowly, over a medium heat, and cook until all the liquid has evaporated.

2 ▲ Remove from the heat and allow to cool slightly. Put the mixture into a food processor or blender and process for 2 minutes, stopping once or twice to loosen the mixture with a spoon.

3 ▲ Scrape the mixture into a large mixing bowl using a wooden spoon. Taking a little of the mixture at a time, shape it into small balls using your hands. You should be able to make about 12 koftas.

4 ▲ Heat the oil in a karahi or deep round-bottomed frying pan (skillet) over a high heat. Turn the heat down slightly and drop the koftas carefully into the oil. Move them around gently to ensure that they cook evenly.

5 When the koftas are lightly browned, remove them from the oil with a slotted spoon and drain on kitchen paper (paper towels). Set to one side.

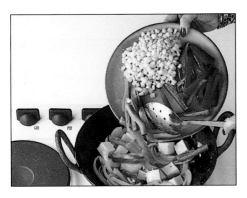

6 ▲ Heat up the oil still remaining in the karahi, and flash fry all the ingredients for the paneer mixture. This should take about 3 minutes over a high heat.

7 ▲ Divide the paneer mixture evenly between 6 individual karahis. Add 2 koftas to each serving, and garnish with mint sprigs and the crushed red chilli, if wished.

Chicken with Pineapple

LOW-FAT RECIPE

This chicken has a delicate tang and is very tender. The pineapple not only tenderizes the chicken but also gives it a slight sweetness.

SERVES 6

INGREDIENTS
225 g/8 oz/1 cup canned pineapple
1 tsp ground cumin
1 tsp ground coriander
1/2 tsp garlic pulp
1 tsp chilli powder
1 tsp salt
2 tbsp natural (plain) low-fat yogurt
1 tbsp chopped fresh coriander (cilantro)
few drops orange food colouring
275 g/10 oz/2 cups chicken, skinned and
    boned
1/2 red (bell) pepper
1/2 yellow or green (bell) pepper
1 large onion
6 cherry tomatoes
1 tbsp vegetable oil

NUTRITIONAL VALUES (per portion)	
Total fat	6.72 g
Saturated fat	1.51 g
Cholesterol	40.63 mg
Energy (kcals/kj)	170/716

2 ▲ In a large mixing bowl, blend together the cumin, ground coriander, garlic, chilli powder, salt, yogurt, fresh coriander (cilantro) and food colouring, if using. Pour in the reserved pineapple juice and mix together.

1 ▲ Drain the pineapple juice into a bowl. Reserve 8 large chunks of pineapple and squeeze the juice from the remaining chunks into the bowl and set aside. You should have about 120 ml/4 fl oz/1/2 cup of pineapple juice.

3 ▲ Cut the chicken into bite-sized cubes, add to the yogurt and spice mixture and leave to marinate for about 1–1 1/2 hours.

4 Cut the (bell) peppers and onion into bite-sized chunks.

5 ▲ Preheat the grill (broiler) to medium. Arrange the chicken pieces, vegetables and reserved pineapple chunks alternately on 6 wooden or metal skewers.

6 ▲ Baste the kebabs (kabobs) with the oil, then place the skewers on a flameproof dish or grill tray. Grill (broil), turning and basting the chicken pieces with the marinade regularly, for about 15 minutes.

7 Once the chicken pieces are cooked, remove them from the grill and serve either with salad or plain boiled rice.

COOK'S TIP

If possible, use a mixture of chicken breast and thigh meat for this recipe.

Chicken and Pasta Balti

This is not a traditional Balti dish, as pasta is not eaten widely in India or Pakistan, however, I have included it here as it is truly delicious! The pomegranate seeds give this dish an unusual tangy flavour.

SERVES 4–6

INGREDIENTS
75 g/3 oz/³/4 cup small pasta shells (the coloured ones look most attractive)
5 tbsp corn oil
4 curry leaves
4 whole dried red chillies
1 large onion, sliced
1 tsp garlic pulp
1 tsp chilli powder
1 tsp shredded ginger
1 tsp crushed pomegranate seeds
1 tsp salt
2 medium tomatoes, chopped
175 g/6 oz/1¹/3 cups chicken, skinned, boned and cubed
225 g/8 oz/1¹/2 cups canned chick-peas (garbanzos), drained

115 g/4 oz/²/3 cup sweetcorn (corn kernels)
50 g/2 oz mange-tout (snow peas), diagonally sliced
1 tbsp chopped fresh coriander (cilantro) (optional)

1 ▲ Cook the pasta in boiling water, following the directions on the package. Add 1 tbsp of the oil to the water to prevent the pasta from sticking together. When it is cooked, drain and set to one side in a sieve (strainer).

2 ▲ Heat the remaining oil in a deep round-bottomed frying pan (skillet) or a large karahi, and add the curry leaves, whole dried chillies and the onion. Fry for about 5 minutes.

3 Add the garlic, chilli powder, ginger, pomegranate seeds, salt and tomatoes. Stir-fry for about 3 minutes.

4 ▲ Next add the chicken, chick-peas (garbanzos), sweetcorn (corn kernels) and mange-tout (snow peas) to the onion mixture. Cook over a medium heat for about 5 minutes, stirring.

5 ▲ Tip in the pasta and stir well. Cook for a further 7–10 minutes until the chicken is cooked through.

6 Serve garnished with the fresh coriander (cilantro) if wished.

Balti Lamb Chops with Potatoes

These chops are marinated before being cooked in a delicious spicy sauce. They make a good appetizer, served with a simple mixed salad.

SERVES 6–8

INGREDIENTS

8 lamb chops (about 50–75 g/2–3 oz each)
2 tbsp olive oil
150 ml/¼ pint/⅔ cup lemon juice
1 tsp salt
1 tbsp chopped fresh mint and coriander (cilantro)
150 ml/¼ pint/⅔ cup corn oil
mint sprigs
lime slices

Sauce

3 tbsp corn oil
8 medium tomatoes, roughly chopped
1 bay leaf
1 tsp garam masala
2 tbsp natural (plain) yogurt
1 tsp garlic pulp
1 tsp chilli powder
1 tsp salt
½ tsp black cumin seeds
3 black peppercorns
2 medium potatoes, peeled, roughly chopped and boiled

1 ▲ Put the chops into a large bowl. Mix together the olive oil, lemon juice, salt and fresh mint and coriander (cilantro). Pour the oil mixture over the chops and rub it in well with your fingers. Leave to marinate for at least 3 hours.

2 ▲ To make the sauce, heat the corn oil in a deep round-bottomed frying pan (skillet) or a karahi. Lower the heat and add the chopped tomatoes. Stir-fry for about 2 minutes. Gradually add the bay leaf, garam masala, yogurt, garlic, chilli powder, salt, black cumin seeds and peppercorns, and stir-fry for a further 2–3 minutes.

3 Lower the heat again and add the cooked potatoes, mixing everything together well. Remove from the heat and set to one side.

4 ▲ Heat 150 ml/¼ pint/⅔ cup corn oil in a separate frying pan. Lower the heat slightly and fry the marinated chops until they are cooked through. This will take about 10–12 minutes. Remove with a slotted spoon and drain the cooked chops on kitchen paper (paper towels).

5 Heat the sauce in the karahi, bringing it to the boil. Add the chops and lower the heat. Simmer for 5–7 minutes.

6 Transfer to a warmed serving dish and garnish with the mint sprigs and lime slices.

Tandoori Masala Spring Lamb Chops

These spicy lean and trimmed lamb chops are marinated for three hours and then cooked in the oven using very little cooking oil. They make an excellent appetizer, served with a salad, and would also serve three as a main course with a rice accompaniment.

SERVES 6

INGREDIENTS
6 spring lamb chops
2 tbsp natural (plain) low-fat yogurt
1 tbsp tomato purée (paste)
2 tsp ground coriander
1 tsp ginger pulp
1 tsp garlic pulp
1 tsp chilli powder
few drops red food colouring (optional)
1 tsp salt
1 tbsp corn oil
3 tbsp lemon juice
oil for basting

Garnish
lettuce leaves (optional)
lime wedges
1 small onion, sliced
fresh coriander (cilantro) sprigs

NUTRITIONAL VALUES (per portion)	
Total fat	7.27 g
Saturated fat	2.50 g
Cholesterol	39.70 mg
Energy (kcals/kj)	116/488

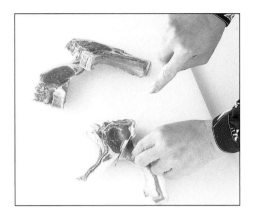

1 ▲ Rinse the chops and pat dry. Trim off any fat.

2 ▲ In a medium bowl, mix together the yogurt, tomato purée (paste), ground coriander, ginger, garlic, chilli powder, food colouring, if using, salt, oil and lemon juice.

3 ▲ Rub this mixture over the chops, using your hands, and leave to marinate for at least 3 hours.

4 ▲ Preheat the oven to 240°C/475°F/ Gas 9. Place the marinated chops in an ovenproof dish.

5 ▲ Using a brush, baste the chops with about 1 tsp of oil and cook in the preheated oven for 15 minutes. Lower the heat to 180°C/350°F/Gas 4 and cook for a further 10–15 minutes.

6 Check to see that the chops are cooked and serve immediately on a bed of lettuce leaves, if wished, and garnish with lime wedges, sliced onion and fresh coriander (cilantro) sprigs.

Vegetable Samosas

Traditional samosa pastry requires a lot of time and hard work but spring roll pastry makes an excellent substitute and is readily available. One packet will make 30 samosas. They can be frozen before or after frying.

SERVES 4–6

INGREDIENTS
1 packet spring roll pastry, thawed and wrapped in a damp dish towel
vegetable oil, for deep-frying

Filling
3 large potatoes, boiled and coarsely mashed
75 g/3 oz/³/4 cup frozen peas, cooked and drained
50 g/2 oz/¹/3 cup canned sweetcorn (corn kernels), drained
1 tsp ground coriander
1 tsp ground cumin
1 tsp mango powder

1 small onion (red if available), finely chopped
salt, to taste
2 fresh green chillies, finely chopped
2 tbsp each, chopped fresh coriander (cilantro) and mint
juice of 1 lemon

1 ▲ Toss all the filling ingredients together in a large mixing bowl until well blended. Adjust seasoning of salt and lemon juice, if necessary.

2 ▲ Using one strip of pastry at a time, place 1 tbsp of the filling mixture at one end of the strip and diagonally fold the pastry to form a triangle.

3 Heat enough oil for deep-frying and fry the samosas in small batches until they are golden brown. Serve hot with Fresh Coriander (Cilantro) Relish or a chilli sauce.

Spicy Omelette

Eggs are packed with nutritional value and make wholesome and delicious dishes. This omelette, cooked with potatoes, onions and a touch of spices, can be put together quickly for an emergency meal.

SERVES 4–6

INGREDIENTS
2 tbsp vegetable oil
1 medium onion, finely chopped
¹/2 tsp ground cumin
1 clove garlic, finely crushed
1 fresh green chilli, finely chopped
few sprigs fresh coriander, chopped
1 firm tomato, chopped
1 small potato, cubed and boiled
25 g/1 oz/2 tbsp cooked peas
25g/1 oz/2 tbsp cooked sweetcorn (corn kernels)

salt and pepper, to taste
2 eggs, beaten
25 g/1 oz grated cheese
1 fresh green chilli, sliced, to garnish (optional)

1 ▲ Heat the oil in a frying pan (skillet) and fry the next 9 ingredients until well blended but the tomato and potato are firm. Season to taste.

2 ▲ Increase the heat and pour in the beaten eggs. Reduce the heat, cover and cook until the bottom layer is brown. Sprinkle with the grated cheese. Place under a hot grill (broiler) and cook until the egg sets and the cheese has melted. Garnish with the fresh chilli, if wished.

Vegetable Samosas (top) and Spicy Omelette

Baked Potato with Spicy Cottage Cheese

Always choose a variety of potato recommended for baking for this recipe, as the texture of the potato should not be too dry. This makes an excellent low-fat snack any time of the day.

SERVES 4

INGREDIENTS
4 medium baking potatoes
225 g/8 oz/1 cup low-fat cottage cheese
2 tsp tomato purée (paste)
1/2 tsp ground cumin
1/2 tsp ground coriander
1/2 tsp chilli powder
1/2 tsp salt
1 tbsp corn oil
1/2 tsp mixed onion and mustard seeds
3 curry leaves
2 tbsp water

Garnish
mixed salad leaves
fresh coriander (cilantro) sprigs
lemon wedges
2 tomatoes, quartered

1 ▲ Preheat the oven to 180°C/350°F/ Gas 4. Wash, pat dry and make a slit in the middle of each potato. Prick the potatoes a few times with a fork, then wrap them individually in foil. Bake in the preheated oven for about 1 hour until soft.

NUTRITIONAL VALUES (per portion)	
Total fat	4.60 g
Saturated fat	0.41 g
Cholesterol	2.81 mg
Energy (kcals/kj)	335/1409

2 Transfer the cottage cheese into a heatproof dish and set aside.

3 ▲ In a separate bowl, mix together the tomato purée (paste), ground cumin, ground coriander, chilli powder and salt.

4 ▲ Heat the corn oil in a small saucepan for about 1 minute. Add the mixed onion and mustard seeds and the curry leaves and tilt the saucepan so the oil covers all the seeds and leaves.

5 When the leaves turn a shade darker and you can smell their beautiful aroma, pour the tomato purée mixture into the saucepan and lower the heat immediately to low. Add the water and mix well.

6 ▲ Cook for a further 1 minute, then pour the spicy tomato mixture onto the cottage cheese and blend everything together well.

7 ▲ Check that the potatoes are cooked right through. Unwrap the potatoes and divide the cottage cheese equally between the 4 potatoes.

8 Garnish with the mixed salad leaves, fresh coriander (cilantro) sprigs, lemon wedges and tomato quarters.

VARIATION

This recipe can also be used as the basis for a tangy vegetable accompaniment to a main meal. Instead of using baked potatoes, boil new potatoes in their skins then cut in half. Add the cooked potatoes to the spicy cottage mixture, mix together well and serve.

Prawns (Shrimp) with Pomegranate Seeds

King prawns (jumbo shrimp) are best for this dish. It makes an impressive appetizer, and is delicious served with a mixed salad.

SERVES 4

INGREDIENTS
1 tsp crushed garlic
1 tsp grated ginger
1 tsp coarsely ground pomegranate seeds
1 tsp ground coriander
1 tsp salt
1 tsp chilli powder
2 tbsp tomato purée (paste)
4 tbsp water
3 tbsp chopped fresh coriander (cilantro)
2 tbsp corn oil
12 large cooked prawns (shrimp)
1 medium onion, sliced into rings

1 Put the garlic, ginger, pomegranate seeds, ground coriander, salt, chilli powder, tomato purée (paste), water and 2 tbsp of the fresh coriander (cilantro) into a bowl. Pour in the oil and blend everything together thoroughly.

2 ▲ Peel and wash the prawns and rinse them gently under running water. Using a sharp knife, make a small slit at the back of each prawn. Open out each prawn to make a butterfly shape.

3 Add the prawns to the spice mixture, making sure they are all well coated. Leave to marinate for about 2 hours.

4 ▲ Meanwhile, cut four squares of foil, about 20 × 20 cm/8 × 8 in. Preheat the oven to 230°C/450°F/Gas 8. When the prawns are ready, place 3 prawns and a few onion rings onto each square of foil, garnishing each with a little fresh coriander, and fold up into little packages. Bake for about 12–15 minutes and open up the foil to serve.

Grilled (Broiled) Prawns (Shrimp)

Prawns (shrimp) are delicious grilled (broiled), especially when they are flavoured with spices. Buy the largest prawns you can find for this dish.

SERVES 4–6

INGREDIENTS
18 large cooked prawns (shrimp)
4 tbsp lemon juice
1 tsp salt
1 tsp chilli powder
1 tsp garlic pulp
1½ tsp soft light brown sugar
3 tbsp corn oil
2 tbsp chopped fresh coriander (cilantro)
1 fresh green chilli, sliced
1 tomato, sliced
1 small onion, cut into rings
lemon wedges

1 ▲ Peel the prawns (shrimp) and rinse them gently under cold water. Using a sharp knife, make a slit at the back of each prawn and open out into a butterfly shape. Put the remaining ingredients, with the exception of the chilli, tomato, onion and lemon wedges, in a bowl and mix together thoroughly.

2 Add the prawns to the spice mixture, making sure they are well coated, and leave to marinate for about 1 hour.

3 Place the green chilli, tomato slices and onion rings in a flameproof dish. Add the prawn mixture and cook under a very hot preheated grill (broiler) for about 10–15 minutes, basting several times with a brush. Serve immediately, garnished with the lemon wedges.

A mixed salad of cucumber, watercress, sweetcorn (corn kernels) and cherry tomatoes, garnished with lemon wedges and onion rings (top) is delicious served with Prawns (Shrimp) with Pomegranate Seeds (centre) and Grilled (Broiled) Prawns (Shrimp).

Poultry Dishes

Chicken is especially good in curries, and even the most subtle blend of spices will produce a deliciously aromatic dish. If you are in a hurry, try one of the Balti recipes; these quick stir-fried dishes are easy to cook at home. If you are entertaining, impress your friends with Khara Masala Balti Chicken — a dry-style curry with whole spices, ginger and fresh coriander.

Balti Chicken

This recipe has a beautifully delicate flavour, and is probably the most popular of all Balti dishes. Choose a young chicken as it will be more flavoursome.

SERVES 4–6

INGREDIENTS
*1–1½ kg/2½–3 lb chicken, skinned and
   cut into 8 pieces*
3 tbsp corn oil
3 medium onions, sliced
3 medium tomatoes, halved and sliced
2.5 cm/1 in cinnamon stick
2 large black cardamom pods
4 black peppercorns
½ tsp black cumin seeds
1 tsp ginger pulp
1 tsp garlic pulp
1 tsp garam masala
1 tsp chilli powder
1 tsp salt
2 tbsp natural (plain) yogurt
4 tbsp lemon juice
2 tbsp chopped fresh coriander (cilantro)
2 fresh green chillies, chopped

I Wash and trim the chicken pieces, and set to one side.

2 ▲ Heat the oil in a large karahi or deep round-bottomed frying pan (skillet). Throw in the onions and fry until they are golden brown. Add the tomatoes and stir well.

3 ▲ Add the cinnamon stick, cardamoms, peppercorns, black cumin seeds, ginger, garlic, garam masala, chilli powder and salt. Lower the heat and stir-fry for 3–5 minutes.

4 ▲ Add the chicken pieces, 2 at a time, and stir-fry for at least 7 minutes or until the spice mixture has completely penetrated the chicken pieces.

5 ▲ Add the yogurt to the chicken and mix well.

6 Lower the heat and cover the pan with a piece of foil, making sure that the foil does not touch the food. Cook very gently for about 15 minutes, checking once to make sure the food is not catching on the bottom of the pan.

7 ▲ Finally, add the lemon juice, fresh coriander (cilantro) and green chillies, and serve at once.

COOK'S TIP

Chicken cooked on the bone is both tender and flavoursome. However, do substitute the whole chicken with 675 g/1½ lb boned and cubed chicken, if wished. The cooking time can be reduced at step 6, too.

Chicken in a Cashew Nut Sauce

LOW-FAT RECIPE

This chicken dish has a deliciously thick and nutty sauce, and it is best served with plain boiled rice.

SERVES 4

INGREDIENTS
2 medium onions
2 tbsp tomato purée (paste)
50 g/2 oz/⅓ cup cashew nuts
1½ tsp garam masala
1 tsp garlic pulp
1 tsp chilli powder
1 tbsp lemon juice
¼ tsp turmeric
1 tsp salt
1 tbsp natural (plain) low-fat yogurt
2 tbsp corn oil
1 tbsp chopped fresh coriander (cilantro)
1 tbsp sultanas (golden raisins)
450 g/1 lb/3¼ cups chicken, skinned, boned and cubed
175 g/6 oz/2½ cups button mushrooms
300 ml/½ pint/1¼ cups water
1 tbsp chopped fresh coriander (cilantro)

NUTRITIONAL VALUES (per portion)

Total fat	14.64 g
Saturated fat	2.87 g
Cholesterol	64.84 mg
Energy (kcals/kj)	280/1176

1 ▲ Cut the onions into quarters and place in a food processor or blender and process for about 1 minute.

2 ▲ Add the tomato purée (paste), cashew nuts, garam masala, garlic, chilli powder, lemon juice, turmeric, salt and yogurt to the processed onions.

3 Process all the ingredients in the food processor for a further 1–1½ minutes.

4 In a saucepan, heat the oil, lower the heat to medium and pour in the spice mixture from the food processor. Fry for about 2 minutes, lowering the heat if necessary.

5 ▲ Add the fresh coriander (cilantro), sultanas (golden raisins) and chicken and continue to stir-fry for a further 1 minute.

6 ▲ Add the mushrooms, pour in the water and bring to a simmer. Cover the saucepan and cook over a low heat for about 10 minutes.

7 ▲ After this time, check to see that the chicken is cooked through and the sauce is thick. Cook for a little longer if necessary.

8 Serve garnished with chopped fresh coriander.

Balti Chicken with Vegetables

In this recipe the chicken and vegetables are cut into strips which makes the dish particularly attractive.

SERVES 4–6

❀❀❀❀❀❀❀❀❀❀❀❀❀❀❀❀❀❀

INGREDIENTS
4 tbsp corn oil
2 medium onions, sliced
4 garlic cloves, thickly sliced
450 g/1 lb/3¼ cups chicken breast, skinned, boned and cut into strips
1 tsp salt
2 tbsp lime juice
3 fresh green chillies, chopped
2 medium carrots, cut into batons

2 medium potatoes, peeled and cut into 1 cm/½ in strips
1 medium courgette (zucchini), cut into batons
4 lime slices
1 tbsp chopped fresh coriander (cilantro)
2 fresh green chillies, cut into strips (optional)

❀❀❀❀❀❀❀❀❀❀❀❀❀❀❀❀❀❀

1 Heat the oil in a large karahi or deep round-bottomed frying pan (skillet). Lower the heat slightly and add the onions. Fry until lightly browned.

2 ▲ Add half the garlic slices and fry for a few seconds before adding the chicken and salt. Cook everything together, stirring, until all the moisture has evaporated and the chicken is lightly browned.

3 ▲ Add the lime juice, green chillies and all the vegetables to the pan. Turn up the heat and add the rest of the garlic. Stir-fry for 7–10 minutes, or until the chicken is cooked through and the vegetables are just tender.

4 Transfer to a serving dish and garnish with the lime slices, fresh coriander (cilantro) and green chilli strips, if wished.

Balti Chilli Chicken

Hot and spicy would be the best way of describing this mouth-watering Balti dish. The smell of the fresh chillies cooking is indescribable!

SERVES 4–6

INGREDIENTS

5 tbsp corn oil
8 large fresh green chillies, slit
½ tsp mixed onion and cumin seeds
4 curry leaves
1 tsp ginger pulp
1 tsp chilli powder
1 tsp ground coriander
1 tsp garlic pulp
1 tsp salt
2 medium onions, chopped
675 g/1½ lb/4⅔ cups chicken, skinned, boned and cubed
1 tbsp lemon juice
1 tbsp roughly chopped fresh mint
1 tbsp roughly chopped fresh coriander (cilantro)
8–10 cherry tomatoes

1 ▲ Heat the oil in a deep round-bottomed frying pan (skillet) or a medium karahi. Lower the heat slightly and add the slit green chillies. Fry until the skin starts to change colour.

2 ▲ Add the onion and cumin seeds, curry leaves, ginger, chilli powder, ground coriander, garlic, salt and onions, and fry for a few seconds, stirring continuously.

3 Add the chicken pieces and stir-fry for 7–10 minutes, or until the chicken is cooked right through.

4 ▼ Sprinkle on the lemon juice and add the mint and coriander (cilantro).

5 Add the cherry tomatoes and serve with Naan or Paratha.

Classic Tandoori Chicken

This is probably the most famous of Indian dishes. Marinate the chicken well and cook in an extremely hot oven for a clay oven-baked taste. If you want authentic "burnt" spots on the chicken, place the dish under a hot grill (broiler) for a few minutes after baking.

SERVES 4–6

INGREDIENTS
1.5 kg/3 lb oven-ready chicken
250 ml/8 fl oz/1 cup natural (plain)
    yogurt, beaten
4 tbsp tandoori masala paste
salt, to taste
6 tbsp ghee
salad leaves, to serve
lemon twist and onion slices, to garnish

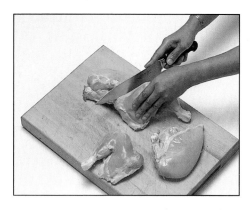

2 ▲ Cut the chicken in half down the centre and through the breast. Cut each piece in half again. Make a few deep gashes diagonally into the flesh. Mix the yogurt with the masala paste and salt. Spread the chicken evenly with the yogurt mixture, spreading some into the gashes. Leave for at least 2 hours, but preferably overnight.

4 ▲ Melt the ghee and pour over the chicken to seal the surface. This helps to keep the centre moist during the roasting period. Cook in the preheated oven for 10 minutes, then remove, leaving the oven on.

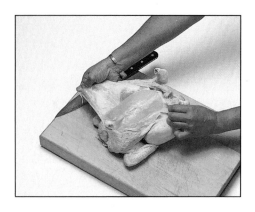

1 ▲ Using a sharp knife or scissors, remove the skin from the chicken and trim off any excess fat. Using a fork, beat the flesh at random.

3 ▲ Preheat the oven to maximum heat. Place the chicken quarters on a wire rack in a deep baking tray. Spread the chicken with any excess marinade, reserve a little for basting halfway through cooking time.

5 ▲ Baste the chicken pieces with the remaining marinade. Return to the oven and switch off the heat. Leave the chicken in the oven for about 15–20 minutes without opening the door. Serve on a bed of salad leaves and garnish with the lemon twist and onion slices.

Balti Chicken in Saffron Sauce

This is a beautifully aromatic chicken dish that is partly cooked in the oven. It contains saffron, the most expensive spice in the world, and is sure to impress your guests.

SERVES 4–6

INGREDIENTS
50 g/2 oz/4 tbsp butter
2 tbsp corn oil
1–1½ kg/2½–3 lb chicken, skinned and cut into 8 pieces
1 medium onion, chopped
1 tsp garlic pulp
½ tsp crushed black peppercorns
½ tsp crushed cardamom pods
¼ tsp ground cinnamon
1½ tsp chilli powder
150 ml/¼ pint/⅔ cup natural (plain) yogurt
50 g/2 oz/½ cup ground almonds
1 tbsp lemon juice
1 tsp salt
1 tsp saffron strands
150 ml/¼ pint/⅔ cup water
150 ml/¼ pint/⅔ cup single (light) cream
2 tbsp chopped fresh coriander (cilantro)

1 ▲ Preheat the oven to 180°C/350°F/ Gas 4. Melt the butter with the oil in a deep round-bottomed frying pan (skillet) or a medium karahi. Add the chicken pieces and fry until lightly browned. This will take about 5 minutes. Remove the chicken using a slotted spoon, leaving behind as much of the fat as possible.

2 ▲ Add the onion to the same pan, and fry over a medium heat. Meanwhile, mix together the garlic, black peppercorns, cardamom, cinnamon, chilli powder, yogurt, ground almonds, lemon juice, salt and saffron strands in a mixing bowl.

3 ▲ When the onions are lightly browned, pour the spice mixture into the pan and stir-fry for about 1 minute.

4 ▲ Add the chicken pieces, and continue to stir-fry for a further 2 minutes. Add the water and bring to a simmer.

5 Transfer the contents of the pan to a casserole dish and cover with a lid, or, if using a karahi, cover with foil. Transfer to the oven and cook for 30–35 minutes.

6 ▲ Once you are sure that the chicken is cooked right through, remove it from the oven. Transfer the chicken to a frying pan and stir in the cream.

7 Reheat gently on the hob for about 2 minutes. Garnish with fresh coriander (cilantro) and serve with Fruity Pullao or plain boiled rice.

COOK'S TIP

There is no substitute for saffron, so don't be tempted to use turmeric instead. It is well worth buying a small amount of saffron – either strands or in powdered form – to create this dish for a special occasion.

Spicy Masala Chicken

These chicken pieces are grilled (broiled) and have a sweet-and-sour taste. They can be served cold with a salad and rice or hot with Masala Mashed Potatoes.

SERVES 6

INGREDIENTS
12 chicken thighs
6 tbsp lemon juice
1 tsp ginger pulp
1 tsp garlic pulp
1 tsp crushed dried red chillies
1 tsp salt
1 tsp soft brown sugar
2 tbsp clear honey
2 tbsp chopped fresh coriander (cilantro)
1 fresh green chilli, finely chopped
2 tbsp vegetable oil
fresh coriander (cilantro) sprigs

1 Prick the chicken thighs with a fork, rinse, pat dry and set aside in a bowl.

2 ▲ In a large mixing bowl, mix together the lemon juice, ginger, garlic, crushed dried red chillies, salt, sugar and honey.

3 Transfer the chicken thighs to the spice mixture and coat well. Set aside for about 45 minutes.

NUTRITIONAL VALUES (per portion)

Total fat	9.20 g
Saturated fat	2.31 g
Cholesterol	73.00 mg
Energy (kcals/kj)	189/795

4 ▲ Preheat the grill (broiler) to medium. Add the fresh coriander (cilantro) and chopped green chilli to the chicken thighs and place them on a flameproof dish.

5 ▲ Pour any remaining marinade over the chicken and baste with the oil, using a pastry brush.

6 Grill (broil) the chicken thighs under the preheated grill for 15–20 minutes, turning and basting occasionally, until cooked through and browned.

7 Transfer to a serving dish and garnish with the fresh coriander sprigs.

Tandoori Chicken

A most popular Indian/Pakistan chicken dish which is cooked in a clay oven called a tandoor, this is extremely popular in the West and appears on the majority of the restaurant menus. Though the authentic tandoori flavour is very difficult to achieve in conventional ovens, this version still makes a very tasty dish.

SERVES 4

INGREDIENTS
4 chicken quarters
175 ml/6 fl oz/³/4 cup natural (plain) low-fat yogurt
1 tsp garam marsala
1 tsp ginger pulp
1 tsp garlic pulp
1¹/2 tsp chilli powder
¹/4 tsp turmeric
1 tsp ground coriander
1 tbsp lemon juice
1 tsp salt
few drops red food colouring
2 tbsp corn oil

Garnish
mixed salad leaves
lime wedges
1 tomato, quartered

1 ▲ Skin, rinse and pat dry the chicken quarters. Make 2 slits into the flesh of each piece, place in a dish and set aside.

NUTRITIONAL VALUES (per portion)	
Total fat	10.64 g
Saturated fat	2.74 g
Cholesterol	81.90 mg
Energy (kcals/kj)	242/1018

2 ▲ Mix together the yogurt, garam marsala, ginger, garlic, chilli powder, turmeric, ground coriander, lemon juice, salt, red colouring and oil, and beat so that all the ingredients are well mixed together.

3 Cover the chicken quarters with the spice mixture and leave to marinate for about 3 hours.

4 ▲ Preheat the oven to 240°C/475°F/ Gas 9. Transfer the chicken pieces to an ovenproof dish.

5 Bake in the preheated oven for 20–25 minutes or until the chicken is cooked right through and browned on top.

6 Remove from the oven, transfer onto a serving dish and garnish with the salad leaves, lime and tomato.

Balti Butter Chicken

Butter Chicken is one of the most popular Balti chicken dishes, especially in the West. Cooked in butter, with aromatic spices, cream and almonds, this mild dish will be enjoyed by everyone. Serve with Colourful Pullao Rice.

SERVES 4–6

INGREDIENTS

150 ml/¼ pint/⅔ cup natural (plain) yogurt
50 g/2 oz/½ cup ground almonds
1½ tsp chilli powder
¼ tsp crushed bay leaves
¼ tsp ground cloves
¼ tsp ground cinnamon
1 tsp garam masala
4 green cardamom pods
1 tsp ginger pulp
1 tsp garlic pulp
400 g/14 oz/2 cups canned tomatoes
1¼ tsp salt
1 kg/2 lb/6½ cups chicken, skinned, boned and cubed
75 g/3 oz/6 tbsp butter
1 tbsp corn oil
2 medium onions, sliced
2 tbsp chopped fresh coriander (cilantro)
4 tbsp single (light) cream
coriander sprigs

1 ▲ Put the yogurt, ground almonds, all the dry spices, ginger, garlic, tomatoes and salt into a mixing bowl and blend together thoroughly.

2 ▲ Put the chicken into a large mixing bowl and pour over the yogurt mixture. Set aside.

3 Melt together the butter and oil in a medium karahi or deep round-bottomed frying pan (skillet). Add the onions and fry for about 3 minutes.

4 ▲ Add the chicken mixture and stir-fry for 7–10 minutes.

5 ▲ Stir in about half of the coriander (cilantro) and mix well.

6 ▲ Pour over the cream and stir in well. Bring to the boil. Serve garnished with the remaining chopped coriander and coriander sprigs.

COOK'S TIP

Substitute natural (plain) yogurt with Greek-style yogurt for an even richer and creamier flavour.

Stuffed Roast Chicken

At one time this dish was only cooked in royal palaces and ingredients varied according to individual chefs. The saffron and the rich stuffing make it a truly royal dish.

SERVES 4–6

INGREDIENTS
1 sachet saffron powder
1/2 tsp ground nutmeg
1 tbsp warm milk
1.5 kg/3 lb whole chicken
6 tbsp ghee
5 tbsp hot water

Stuffing
3 medium onions, finely chopped
2 fresh green chillies, chopped
50 g/2 oz/1/3 cup sultanas (golden raisins)
50 g/2 oz/1/2 cup ground almonds
50 g/2 oz dried apricots, soaked until soft
3 hard-boiled eggs, coarsely chopped
salt, to taste

Masala
4 sprigs spring onions (scallions), chopped
2 cloves garlic, crushed
1 tsp five-spice powder
4–6 green cardamom pods
1/2 tsp turmeric
1 tsp freshly ground black pepper
2 tbsp natural (plain) yogurt
50 g/2 oz/1 cup desiccated (shredded) coconut, toasted

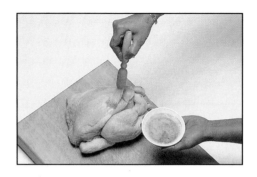

1 ▲ Mix together the saffron, nutmeg and milk. Brush the inside of the chicken with the mixture and carefully spread some over the skin. Heat 4 tbsp of the ghee in a large frying pan (skillet) and fry the chicken on all sides to seal it. Remove and keep warm.

2 ▲ To make the stuffing, in the same ghee, fry the onions, chillies, and sultanas (golden raisins) for 2–3 minutes. Remove from the heat, allow to cool and add the ground almonds, apricots, chopped eggs and salt. Toss the mixture well, then stuff the chicken.

3 ▲ Heat the remaining ghee in a large heavy pan and gently fry all the masala ingredients except the coconut for 2–3 minutes. Add the water. Place the chicken on the bed of masala, cover the pan and cook until the chicken is tender. Remove the chicken from the pan and set aside, keeping warm.

4 ▲ Return the pan to the heat and cook to reduce excess fluids in the masala. When the mixture thickens, pour over the chicken. Sprinkle with toasted coconut and serve hot.

Chicken Curry

Chicken curry is always popular whether served at a family dinner or a banquet. This version is cooked covered, giving a thin consistency. If you would prefer it thick, cook uncovered for the last 15 minutes.

SERVES 4–6

INGREDIENTS
4 tbsp vegetable oil
4 cloves
4–6 green cardamom pods
1 piece cinnamon stick, 5 cm/2 in long
3 whole star anise
6–8 curry leaves
1 large onion, finely chopped
1 piece fresh ginger, 5 cm/2 in long, crushed
4 cloves garlic, crushed
4 tbsp mild curry paste
1 tsp turmeric
1 tsp five-spice powder
1.5 kg/3 lb chicken, skinned and jointed
400 g/14 oz canned tomatoes, chopped
115 g/4 oz creamed coconut
½ tsp sugar
salt, to taste
50 g/2 oz/2 cups fresh coriander (cilantro), chopped

2 ▲ Add the onion, ginger and garlic and fry until the onion turns brown. Add the curry paste, turmeric and five-spice powder and fry until the oil separates.

4 ▲ Add the chopped tomatoes and the creamed coconut. Simmer gently until the coconut dissolves. Mix well and add the sugar and salt. Fold in the chopped fresh coriander (cilantro), then reheat and serve hot.

3 ▲ Add the chicken pieces and mix well. When all the pieces are evenly sealed, cover and cook until the meat is nearly done.

1 ▲ Heat the oil in a pan and fry the cloves, cardamoms, cinnamon stick, star anise and curry leaves until the cloves swell and the curry leaves are slightly burnt.

Balti Chicken with Lentils

This is rather an unusual combination of flavours, but I do recommend you try it. The mango powder gives a delicious tangy flavour to this spicy dish.

SERVES 4–6

INGREDIENTS
75 g/3 oz/½ cup chana dhal (split yellow lentils)
4 tbsp corn oil
2 medium leeks, chopped
6 large dried red chillies
4 curry leaves
1 tsp mustard seeds
2 tsp mango powder
2 medium tomatoes, chopped
½ tsp chilli powder
1 tsp ground coriander
1 tsp salt
450 g/1 lb/3¼ cups chicken, skinned, boned and cubed
1 tbsp chopped fresh coriander (cilantro)

I Wash the lentils carefully and remove any stones.

2 ▲ Put the lentils into a saucepan with enough water to cover, and boil for about 10 minutes until they are soft but not mushy. Drain and set to one side in a bowl.

3 ▲ Heat the oil in a medium karahi or deep round-bottomed frying pan (skillet). Lower the heat slightly and throw in the leeks, dried red chillies, curry leaves and mustard seeds. Stir-fry gently for a few minutes.

4 ▲ Add the mango powder, tomatoes, chilli powder, ground coriander, salt and chicken, and stir-fry for 7–10 minutes.

5 ▲ Mix in the cooked lentils and fry for a further 2 minutes, or until you are sure that the chicken is cooked right through.

6 Garnish with fresh coriander (cilantro) and serve with Paratha.

COOK'S TIP

Chana dhal, a split yellow lentil, is available from Asian stores. However, split yellow peas are a good substitute.

Hot Chicken Curry

This curry has a nice thick sauce, and I make it using red and green (bell) peppers for extra colour. It can be served with either Wholemeal (Whole-Wheat) Chapatis or plain boiled rice.

SERVES 4

INGREDIENTS
2 tbsp corn oil
¼ tsp fenugreek seeds
¼ tsp onion seeds
2 medium onions, chopped
½ tsp garlic pulp
½ tsp ginger pulp
1 tsp ground coriander
1 tsp chilli powder
1 tsp salt
400 g/14 oz/1¾ cups canned tomatoes
2 tbsp lemon juice
350 g/12 oz/2½ cups chicken, skinned, boned and cubed
2 tbsp chopped fresh coriander (cilantro)
3 fresh green chillies, chopped
½ red (bell) pepper, cut into chunks
½ green (bell) pepper, cut into chunks
fresh coriander (cilantro) sprigs

NUTRITIONAL VALUES (per portion)	
Total fat	9.83 g
Saturated fat	2.03 g
Cholesterol	48.45 mg
Energy (kcals/kj)	205/861

1 ▲ In a medium saucepan, heat the oil and fry the fenugreek and onion seeds until they turn a shade darker. Add the chopped onions, garlic and ginger and fry for about 5 minutes until the onions turn golden brown. Lower the heat to very low.

2 ▲ Meanwhile, in a separate bowl, mix together the ground coriander, chilli powder, salt, tomatoes and lemon juice.

3 ▲ Pour this mixture into the saucepan and turn up the heat to medium. Stir-fry for about 3 minutes.

4 ▲ Add the chicken pieces and stir-fry for 5–7 minutes.

5 ▲ Add the fresh coriander (cilantro), green chillies and the sliced (bell) peppers. Lower the heat, cover the saucepan and let this simmer for about 10 minutes until the chicken is cooked.

6 Serve hot, garnished with fresh coriander sprigs.

COOK'S TIP

For a milder version of this delicious curry, simply omit some or all of the fresh green chillies.

Moghul-Style Chicken

This delicate curry, Moghlai Murgh, can be served as an appetizer followed by spicier curries and rice. Saffron is crucial to the flavour, but as it is very expensive save this dish for special occasions.

SERVES 4–6

INGREDIENTS

2 eggs, beaten with salt and pepper
4 chicken breasts, rubbed with a little garam masala
6 tbsp ghee
1 large onion, finely chopped
1 piece fresh ginger, 5 cm/2 in long, finely crushed
4 cloves garlic, finely crushed
4 cloves
4 green cardamom pods
1 piece cinnamon stick, 5 cm/2 in long
2 bay leaves
15–20 strands of saffron
150 ml/¼ pint/⅔ cup natural (plain) yogurt, beaten with 1 tsp cornflour (cornstarch)
salt, to taste
5 tbsp double (heavy) cream
50 g/2 oz/½ cup ground almonds

1 ▲ Brush the chicken breasts with the beaten eggs. In a frying pan (skillet), heat the ghee and fry the chicken. Remove and keep warm.

3 ▲ Return the chicken mixture to the pan with any juices and gently cook until the chicken is tender. Adjust the seasoning if necessary.

2 ▲ In the same ghee, fry the onion, ginger, garlic, cloves, cardamoms, cinnamon and bay leaves. When the onion turns golden, remove the pan from the heat, allow to cool a little and add the saffron and yogurt. Mix well to prevent the yogurt from curdling.

4 ▲ Just before serving, fold in the cream and ground almonds. Serve hot.

Chicken in a Hot Red Sauce

In India, small chickens are used for this dish and served as an individual appetizer with chapatis. If you wish to serve it as a starter, use 4 poussins instead of chicken joints. Skin them first and make small gashes with a sharp knife to allow the spices to seep in.

SERVES 4–6

INGREDIENTS

4 tsp kashmiri masala paste
4 tbsp tomato ketchup
1 tsp Worcestershire sauce
1 tsp five-spice powder
salt, to taste
1 tsp sugar
8 chicken joints, skinned but not boned
3 tbsp vegetable oil
1 piece fresh ginger, 5 cm/2 in long, finely shredded
4 cloves garlic, finely crushed
juice of 1 lemon
few fresh coriander (cilantro) leaves, finely chopped

1 ▲ To make the marinade, mix together the kashmiri masala, tomato ketchup, Worcestershire sauce, five-spice powder, salt and sugar. Allow to rest in a warm place until the sugar has dissolved.

2 ▲ Rub the chicken pieces with the marinade and allow to rest for a further 2 hours, or overnight if possible.

3 ▲ Heat the oil in a frying pan (skillet) and fry half the ginger and all the garlic until golden brown. Add the chicken pieces, and fry without overlapping until both sides are sealed. Cover and cook until the chicken is nearly tender and the sauce clings with the oil separating.

4 ▲ Sprinkle the chicken with the lemon juice, remaining ginger and fresh coriander (cilantro). Mix well, reheat and serve hot.

Balti Baby Chicken in Tamarind Sauce

The tamarind in this recipe gives the dish a sweet-and-sour flavour; this is also quite a hot Balti.

SERVES 4–6

❖❖❖❖❖❖❖❖❖❖❖❖❖❖❖❖❖❖❖❖

INGREDIENTS
4 tbsp tomato ketchup
1 tbsp tamarind paste
4 tbsp water
1¹/₂ tsp chilli powder
1¹/₂ tsp salt
1 tbsp sugar
1¹/₂ tsp ginger pulp
1¹/₂ tsp garlic pulp
2 tbsp desiccated (shredded) coconut
2 tbsp sesame seeds
1 tsp poppy seeds
1 tsp ground cumin
1¹/₂ tsp ground coriander
2 × 450 g/1 lb baby chickens, skinned and
    cut into 6–8 pieces each
5 tbsp corn oil
8 tbsp curry leaves
¹/₂ tsp onion seeds
3 large dried red chillies
¹/₂ tsp fenugreek seeds
10–12 cherry tomatoes
3 tbsp chopped fresh coriander (cilantro)
2 fresh green chillies, chopped

❖❖❖❖❖❖❖❖❖❖❖❖❖❖❖❖❖❖❖❖

I ▲ Put the tomato ketchup, tamarind paste and water into a large mixing bowl and use a fork to blend everything together.

2 ▲ Add the chilli powder, salt, sugar, ginger, garlic, coconut, sesame and poppy seeds, ground cumin and ground coriander to the mixture.

3 ▲ Add the chicken pieces and stir until they are well coated with the spice mixture. Set to one side.

4 ▲ Heat the oil in a deep round-bottomed frying pan (skillet) or a large karahi. Add the curry leaves, onion seeds, dried red chillies and fenugreek seeds and fry for about 1 minute.

5 ▲ Lower the heat to medium and add the chicken pieces, along with their sauce, 2 or 3 pieces at a time, mixing as you go. When all the pieces are in the pan, stir them around well using a slotted spoon.

6 Simmer gently for about 12–15 minutes, or until the chicken is thoroughly cooked.

7 ▲ Finally, add the tomatoes, fresh coriander (cilantro) and green chillies, and serve with Fried Rice with Cashew Nuts, if wished.

Chicken with Green Mango

Green, unripe mango is used for making various dishes on the Indian sub-continent, including pickles, chutneys and some meat, chicken and vegetable dishes. This is a fairly simple chicken dish to prepare and is served with rice and dhal.

SERVES 4

INGREDIENTS

1 medium green (unripe) mango
450 g/1 lb/3¼ cups chicken, skinned, boned and cubed
¼ tsp onion seeds
1 tsp ginger pulp
½ tsp garlic pulp
1 tsp chilli powder
¼ tsp turmeric
1 tsp salt
1 tsp ground coriander
2 tbsp corn oil
2 medium onions, sliced
4 curry leaves
300 ml/½ pint/1¼ cups water
2 medium tomatoes, quartered
2 fresh green chillies, chopped
2 tbsp chopped fresh coriander (cilantro)

NUTRITIONAL VALUES (per portion)	
Total fat	11.03 g
Saturated fat	2.43 g
Cholesterol	64.12 mg
Energy (kcals/kj)	269/1131

VARIATION

A good, firm cooking apple can be used instead of green mango, if wished. Prepare and cook in exactly the same way.

1 ▲ To prepare the mango, peel the skin and slice the flesh thickly. Discard the stone (seed) from the middle. Place the mango slices in a small bowl, cover and set aside.

2 ▲ Place the chicken cubes in a bowl and add the onion seeds, ginger, garlic, chilli powder, turmeric, salt and ground coriander. Mix the spices into the chicken and add half the mango slices to this mixture as well.

3 ▲ In a medium saucepan, heat the oil and fry the sliced onions until golden brown. Add the curry leaves.

4 ▲ Gradually add the chicken pieces, stirring all the time.

5 ▲ Pour in the water, lower the heat and cook for about 12–15 minutes, stirring occasionally, until the chicken is cooked through and the water has been absorbed.

6 ▲ Add the remaining mango slices, the tomatoes, green chillies and fresh coriander (cilantro) and serve hot.

Chicken and Tomato Balti

If you like tomatoes, you will love this chicken recipe. It makes a semi-dry Balti and is good served with a lentil dish and plain boiled rice.

SERVES 4

INGREDIENTS
4 tbsp corn oil
6 curry leaves
1/2 tsp mixed onion and mustard seeds
8 medium tomatoes, sliced
1 tsp ground coriander
1 tsp chilli powder
1 tsp salt
1 tsp ground cumin
1 tsp garlic pulp
675 g/1 1/2 lb/4 2/3 cups chicken, skinned, boned and cubed
150 ml/1/4 pint/2/3 cup water
1 tbsp sesame seeds, roasted
1 tbsp chopped fresh coriander (cilantro)

1 ▲ Heat the oil in a deep round-bottomed frying pan (skillet) or a medium karahi. Add the curry leaves and mixed onion and mustard seeds and stir well.

2 ▲ Lower the heat slightly and add the tomatoes.

3 ▲ While the tomatoes are gently cooking, mix together the ground coriander, chilli powder, salt, ground cumin and garlic in a bowl. Tip the spices onto the tomatoes.

4 ▲ Add the chicken pieces and stir together well. Stir-fry for about 5 minutes.

5 Pour on the water and continue cooking, stirring occasionally, until the sauce thickens and the chicken is cooked through.

6 ▲ Sprinkle the sesame seeds and fresh coriander (cilantro) over the top of the dish and serve.

COOK'S TIP

Sesame seeds are available from Asian and health food stores. There are two types — unroasted seeds, which are white, and roasted ones, which are lightly browned. To roast sesame seeds at home, simply tip a quantity into a frying pan (skillet) over a high heat for about 1 minute. Shake the pan constantly to prevent the seeds burning. Use immediately or store in a screw-topped jar.

Chicken in Spicy Onions

Murgh Do Piyaza is one of the few dishes of India in which onions appear prominently. Chunky onion slices infused with toasted cumin seeds and shredded ginger add a delicious contrast to the flavour of the chicken.

SERVES 4–6

INGREDIENTS
1.5 kg/3 lb chicken, jointed and skinned
1/2 tsp turmeric
1/2 tsp chilli powder
salt, to taste
4 tbsp oil
4 small onions, finely chopped
175 g/6 oz/6 cups fresh coriander
    (cilantro), coarsely chopped
1 piece fresh ginger, 5 cm/2 in long, finely
    shredded
2 fresh green chillies, finely chopped
2 tsp cumin seeds, dry-roasted
5 tbsp natural (plain) yogurt
5 tbsp double (heavy) cream
1/2 tsp cornflour (cornstarch)

1 ▲ Rub the chicken joints with the turmeric, chilli powder and salt. Heat the oil in a frying pan (skillet) and fry the chicken pieces in batches until both sides are sealed. Remove and keep warm.

2 ▲ Reheat the oil and add 3 of the chopped onions, most of the fresh coriander (cilantro), half the ginger, the green chillies and the cumin seeds and fry until the onions are translucent. Return the chicken to the pan with any juices and mix well. Cover and cook gently for 15 minutes.

3 ▲ Remove the pan from the heat and allow to cool a little. Mix together the yogurt, cream and cornflour (cornstarch) and gradually fold into the chicken, mixing well.

4 ▲ Return the pan to the heat and gently cook until the chicken is tender. Just before serving, stir in the reserved onion, coriander and ginger. Serve hot.

Hot Sweet-and-Sour Duck Casserole

This recipe can be made with any game bird, or even rabbit. It is a distinctively sweet, sour and hot dish best eaten with rice as an accompaniment.

SERVES 4–6

INGREDIENTS
1.5 kg/3 lb duck, jointed and skinned
4 bay leaves
3 tbsp salt
5 tbsp vegetable oil
juice of 5 lemons
8 medium-sized onions, finely chopped
50 g/2 oz garlic, crushed
50 g/2 oz chilli powder
300 ml/½ pint/1¼ cups pickling vinegar
115 g/4 oz fresh ginger, finely sliced or shredded
115 g/4 oz/½ cup sugar
50 g/2 oz garam masala

1 ▲ Place the duck, bay leaves and salt in a large pan and cover with cold water. Bring to the boil then simmer for 30–45 minutes, or until the duck is fully cooked. Remove the pieces of duck and keep warm. Reserve the liquid as a base for stock or soups.

2 ▲ In a large pan, heat the oil and lemon juice until it reaches smoking point. Add the onions, garlic and chilli powder and fry the onions until they are golden brown.

3 ▲ Add the vinegar, ginger and sugar and simmer until the sugar dissolves and the oil has separated from the masala.

4 ▲ Return the duck to the pan and add the garam masala. Mix well, then reheat until the masala clings to the pieces of duck and the sauce is thick. Adjust the seasoning if necessary. If you prefer a thinner sauce, add a little of the reserved stock.

Khara Masala Balti Chicken

Whole spices (khara) are used in this recipe, giving it a wonderfully rich flavour. This is a dry dish so it is best served with Raita and Paratha.

SERVES 4

INGREDIENTS
3 curry leaves
1/4 tsp mustard seeds
1/4 tsp fennel seeds
1/4 tsp onion seeds
1/2 tsp crushed dried red chillies
1/2 tsp white cumin seeds
1/4 tsp fenugreek seeds
1/2 tsp crushed pomegranate seeds
1 tsp salt
1 tsp shredded ginger
3 garlic cloves, sliced
4 tbsp corn oil
4 fresh green chillies, slit
1 large onion, sliced
1 medium tomato, sliced
675 g/1 1/2 lb/4 2/3 cups chicken, skinned, boned and cubed
1 tbsp chopped fresh coriander (cilantro)

I ▲ Mix together the curry leaves, mustard seeds, fennel seeds, onion seeds, crushed red chillies, cumin seeds, fenugreek seeds, crushed pomegranate seeds and salt in a large bowl.

2 ▲ Add the shredded ginger and garlic cloves.

3 ▲ Heat the oil in a medium karahi or deep round-bottomed frying pan (skillet). Add the spice mixture and throw in the green chillies.

4 ▲ Tip in the onion and stir-fry over a medium heat for 5–7 minutes.

5 ▲ Finally add the tomato and chicken pieces, and cook over a medium heat for about 7 minutes. The chicken should be cooked through and the sauce reduced.

6 ▲ Stir everything together over the heat for a further 3–5 minutes, and **serve** garnished with chopped fresh coriander (cilantro).

Karahi Chicken with Mint

LOW-FAT RECIPE

For this tasty dish, the chicken is first boiled before being quickly stir-fried in a little oil, to ensure that it is cooked through despite the short cooking time.

SERVES 4

INGREDIENTS
275 g/10 oz/2 cups chicken breast fillet, skinned and cut into strips
300 ml/½ pint/1¼ cups water
2 tbsp soya oil
2 small bunches spring onions (scallions), roughly chopped
1 tsp shredded fresh ginger
1 tsp crushed dried red chilli
2 tbsp lemon juice
1 tbsp chopped fresh coriander (cilantro)
1 tbsp chopped fresh mint
3 tomatoes, seeded and roughly chopped
1 tsp salt
mint and coriander (cilantro) sprigs

NUTRITIONAL VALUES (per portion)	
Total fat	8.20 g
Saturated fat	1.57 g
Cholesterol	30.42 mg
Energy (kcals/kj)	155/649

1 ▲ Put the chicken and water into a saucepan, bring to the boil and lower the heat to medium. Cook for about 10 minutes or until the water has evaporated and the chicken is cooked. Remove from the heat and set aside.

2 Heat the oil in a frying pan (skillet) or saucepan and stir-fry the spring onions (scallions) for about 2 minutes until soft.

3 ▲ Add the boiled chicken strips and stir-fry for about 3 minutes over a medium heat.

4 ▲ Gradually add the ginger, dried chilli, lemon juice, fresh coriander (cilantro), fresh mint, tomatoes and salt and gently stir to blend all the flavours together.

5 Transfer to a serving dish and garnish with the fresh mint and coriander sprigs.

Karahi Chicken with Fresh Fenugreek

LOW-FAT RECIPE

Fresh fenugreek is a flavour that not many people are familiar with and this recipe is a good introduction to this delicious herb.

SERVES 4

INGREDIENTS
*115 g/4 oz/³/4 cup chicken thigh meat,
    skinned and cut into strips*
*115 g/4 oz/³/4 cup chicken breast fillet, cut
    into strips*
1/2 tsp garlic pulp
1 tsp chilli powder
1/2 tsp salt
2 tsp tomato purée (paste)
2 tbsp soya oil
1 bunch fenugreek leaves
1 tbsp fresh chopped coriander (cilantro)
300 ml/1/2 pint/1 1/4 cups water

NUTRITIONAL VALUES (per portion)	
Total fat	8.15 g
Saturated fat	1.64 g
Cholesterol	32.48 mg
Energy (kcals/kj)	128/536

3 Heat the oil in a large saucepan. Lower the heat and add the tomato purée and spice mixture.

4 ▲ Add the chicken pieces and stir-fry for 5–7 minutes. Lower the heat further.

5 ▲ Add the fenugreek leaves and fresh coriander (cilantro). Continue to stir-fry for 5–7 minutes.

6 Pour in the water, cover and cook for about 5 minutes and serve hot with rice or Wholemeal (Whole-Wheat) Chapatis.

COOK'S TIP

When preparing fresh fenugreek, use only the leaves and discard the stems which are very bitter in flavour.

I ▲ Bring a saucepan of water to the boil, add the chicken strips and cook for about 5–7 minutes. Drain and set aside.

2 ▲ In a mixing bowl, combine the garlic, chilli powder and salt with the tomato purée (paste).

Sweet-and-Sour Balti Chicken

This dish combines a sweet-and-sour flavour with a creamy texture. It is delicious served with Colourful Pullao Rice or Naan.

SERVES 4

INGREDIENTS

3 tbsp tomato purée (paste)
2 tbsp Greek-style yogurt
1½ tsp garam masala
1 tsp chilli powder
1 tsp garlic pulp
2 tbsp mango chutney
1 tsp salt
½ tsp sugar (optional)
4 tbsp corn oil
675 g/1½ lb/4⅔ cups chicken, skinned, boned and cubed
150 ml/¼ pint/⅔ cup water
2 fresh green chillies, chopped
2 tbsp chopped fresh coriander (cilantro)
2 tbsp single (light) cream

1 ▲ Blend together the tomato purée (paste), yogurt, garam masala, chilli powder, garlic, mango chutney, salt and sugar (if using) in a medium mixing bowl.

2 ▲ Heat the oil in a deep round-bottomed frying pan (skillet) or a large karahi. Lower the heat slightly and pour in the spice mixture. Bring to the boil and cook for about 2 minutes, stirring occasionally.

3 ▲ Add the chicken pieces and stir until they are well coated.

4 Add the water to thin the sauce slightly. Continue cooking for 5–7 minutes, or until the chicken is tender.

5 ▲ Finally add the fresh chillies, coriander (cilantro) and cream, and cook for a further 2 minutes until the chicken is cooked through.

Balti Chicken Pasanda

Pasanda dishes are firm favourites in Pakistan, but they are also becoming well known in the West.

SERVES 4

✳✳✳✳✳✳✳✳✳✳✳✳✳✳✳✳✳✳✳✳

INGREDIENTS
4 tbsp Greek-style yogurt
½ tsp black cumin seeds
4 cardamom pods
6 whole black peppercorns
2 tsp garam masala
2.5 cm/1 in cinnamon stick
1 tbsp ground almonds
1 tsp garlic pulp
1 tsp ginger pulp
1 tsp chilli powder
1 tsp salt
675 g/1½ lb/4⅔ cups chicken, skinned, boned and cubed
5 tbsp corn oil
2 medium onions, diced
3 fresh green chillies, chopped
2 tbsp chopped fresh coriander (cilantro)
120 ml/4 fl oz/½ cup single (light) cream

✳✳✳✳✳✳✳✳✳✳✳✳✳✳✳✳✳✳✳✳

3 ▲ Pour in the chicken mixture and stir until it is well blended with the onions.

4 ▲ Cook over a medium heat for 12–15 minutes or until the sauce thickens and the chicken is cooked through.

5 ▲ Add the green chillies and fresh coriander (cilantro), and pour in the cream. Bring to the boil and serve garnished with more coriander, if wished.

COOK'S TIP

✳✳✳✳✳✳✳✳✳✳✳✳✳✳✳✳✳✳✳✳

This Balti dish has a lovely thick sauce and is especially good served with one of the rice dishes from this book.

1 ▲ Mix the yogurt, cumin seeds, cardamoms, peppercorns, garam masala, cinnamon stick, ground almonds, garlic, ginger, chilli powder and salt in a medium mixing bowl. Add the chicken pieces and leave to marinate for about 2 hours.

2 Heat the oil in a large karahi or deep round-bottomed frying pan (skillet). Throw in the onions and fry for 2–3 minutes.

Boiled Egg Curry

This dish is usually served with a biryani or pullao but it is equally good with Fried Whole Fish.

SERVES 3–6

INGREDIENTS
2 tsp white poppy seeds
2 tsp white sesame seeds
2 tsp whole coriander seeds
2 tbsp desiccated (shredded) coconut
350 ml/12 fl oz/1½ cups tomato juice
2 tsp gram flour (besan)
1 tsp ginger pulp
1 tsp chilli powder
¼ tsp asafoetida
salt, to taste
1 tsp sugar
6 hard-boiled eggs, halved
2 tbsp sesame oil

1 tsp cumin seeds
4 dried red chillies
6–8 curry leaves
4 cloves garlic, finely sliced

1 ▲ Heat a frying pan (skillet) and dry-fry the poppy, sesame and coriander seeds for 3–4 minutes. Add the desiccated (shredded) coconut and dry-fry until it browns. Cool and grind the ingredients together using a pestle and mortar or a food processor.

2 Take a little of the tomato juice and mix with the gram flour (besan) to a smooth paste. Add the ginger, chilli powder, asafoetida, salt and sugar and the ground spices. Add the remaining tomato juice, place in a saucepan and simmer gently for 10 minutes.

3 ▲ Add the hard-boiled eggs and cover with the sauce. Heat the oil in a frying pan and fry the remaining ingredients until the chillies turn dark brown. Pour the spices and oil over the egg curry, fold the ingredients together and reheat. Serve hot.

Eggs Baked on Chipsticks

Parsis love eggs, and have developed a variety of unique egg-based dishes such as this one.

SERVES 3–6

INGREDIENTS
225 g/8 oz ready-salted chipsticks
2 fresh green chillies, finely chopped
few fresh coriander (cilantro) leaves, finely chopped
¼ tsp turmeric
4 tbsp vegetable oil
5 tbsp water
6 eggs
salt and freshly ground black pepper, to taste
spring onion (scallion) tassles, to garnish

1 In a bowl, mix the chipsticks, chillies, coriander and turmeric. Heat 2 tbsp of the oil in a small non-stick frying pan (skillet). Add the chipstick mixture and water. Cook until the chipsticks have softened, then fry without stirring until crisp.

2 ▲ Place a plate over the frying pan, holding them tightly together turn the pan over. Remove the pan from the plate. Heat the remaining oil in the pan and slide the pancake back in and brown the other side.

3 ▲ Gently break the eggs on to the pancake, cover the frying pan and allow the eggs to set over a low heat. Season and cook until the base is crisp. Serve hot, garnished with spring onion (scallion) tassles.

Boiled Egg Curry (top) and Eggs Baked on Chipsticks

Meat Dishes

Lamb is the favourite Indian meat and there are lots of recipes to choose from here. Try Balti-style lamb kebabs or lamb koftas, or go for the more traditional Lamb with Spinach. For devotees of really fiery hot curries, Kashmiri-Style Lamb has the perfect hot chilli taste, while Moghul-style Roast Lamb will make a spectacular – and spicy – Sunday lunch.

Balti Lamb Tikka

This is a traditional tikka recipe, in which the lamb is marinated in yogurt and spices. The lamb is usually cut into cubes, but the cooking time can be halved by cutting it into strips instead, as I have done in this recipe.

SERVES 4

INGREDIENTS

450 g/1 lb lamb, cut into strips
175 ml/6 fl oz/³⁄4 cup natural (plain) yogurt
1 tsp ground cumin
1 tsp ground coriander
1 tsp chilli powder
1 tsp garlic pulp
1 tsp salt
1 tsp garam masala
2 tbsp chopped fresh coriander (cilantro)
2 tbsp lemon juice
2 tbsp corn oil
1 tbsp tomato purée (tomato paste)

1 large green (bell) pepper, seeded and sliced
3 large fresh red chillies

1 ▲ Put the lamb strips, yogurt, ground cumin, ground coriander, chilli powder, garlic, salt, garam masala, fresh coriander (cilantro) and lemon juice into a large mixing bowl and stir thoroughly. Set to one side for at least 1 hour to marinate.

2 ▲ Heat the oil in a deep round-bottomed frying pan (skillet) or a medium karahi. Lower the heat slightly and add the tomato purée (paste).

3 ▲ Add the lamb strips to the pan, a few at a time, leaving any excess marinade behind in the bowl.

4 Cook the lamb, stirring frequently, for 7–10 minutes or until it is well browned.

5 ▲ Finally, add the green (bell) pepper slices and the whole red chillies. Heat through, checking that the lamb is cooked through, and serve.

Balti Minced (Ground) Lamb with Potatoes and Fenugreek

The combination of lamb with fresh fenugreek works very well in this dish, which is delicious accompanied by plain boiled rice and mango pickle. Only use the fenugreek leaves, as the stalks can be rather bitter. This dish is traditionally served with rice.

SERVES 4

INGREDIENTS

450 g/1 lb lean minced (ground) lamb
1 tsp ginger pulp
1 tsp garlic pulp
1½ tsp chilli powder
1 tsp salt
¼ tsp turmeric
3 tbsp corn oil
2 medium onions, sliced
2 medium potatoes, peeled, par-boiled and roughly diced
1 bunch fresh fenugreek, chopped
2 tomatoes, chopped
50 g/2 oz/½ cup frozen peas
2 tbsp chopped fresh coriander (cilantro)
3 fresh red chillies, seeded and sliced

1 ▲ Put the minced (ground) lamb, ginger, garlic, chilli powder, salt and turmeric into a large bowl, and mix together thoroughly. Set to one side.

2 Heat the oil in a deep round-bottomed frying pan (skillet) or a medium karahi. Throw in the onion and fry for about 5 minutes until golden brown.

3 ▲ Add the minced lamb and stir-fry over a medium heat for 5–7 minutes.

4 ▲ Stir in the potatoes, chopped fenugreek, tomatoes and peas and cook for a further 5–7 minutes, stirring continuously.

5 Just before serving, stir in the fresh coriander (cilantro) and garnish with fresh red chillies.

Moghul-Style Roast Lamb

This superb dish is just one of many fine examples of the fabulous rich food once enjoyed by Moghul emperors. Try it as a variation to the roast beef.

SERVES 4–6

INGREDIENTS
4 large onions, chopped
4 cloves garlic
1 piece fresh ginger, 5 cm/2 in long, chopped
3 tbsp ground almonds
2 tsp ground cumin
2 tsp ground coriander
2 tsp turmeric
2 tsp garam masala
4–6 fresh green chillies
juice of 1 lemon
salt, to taste
300 ml/½ pint/1¼ cups natural (plain) yogurt, beaten
1.8 kg/4 lb leg of lamb
8–10 cloves
4 firm tomatoes, halved and grilled, to serve
watercress, to garnish
1 tbsp flaked (slivered) almonds, to garnish

2 ▲ Remove most of the fat and skin from the lamb. Using a sharp knife, make deep pockets above the bone at each side of the thick end. Make deep diagonal gashes on both sides.

3 ▲ Push the cloves into the leg of lamb at random.

1 ▲ Place the first 11 ingredients in a food processor and blend to a smooth paste. Gradually add the yogurt and blend until smooth. Grease a large, deep baking tray and preheat the oven to 190°C/375°F/Gas 5.

4 ▲ Place the lamb on the baking tray and push some of the spice mixture into the pockets and gashes.

5 ▲ Spread the remaining spice mixture evenly all over the lamb. Loosely cover the whole tray with foil. Roast in the preheated oven for 2–2½ hours or until the lamb is cooked, removing the foil for the last 10 minutes of cooking time.

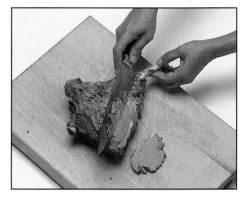

6 ▲ Remove from the oven and allow to rest for 10 minutes before carving. Serve with grilled tomatoes, garnished with watercress and garnish the joint with the flaked (slivered) almonds.

Lamb with Spinach

Lamb with Spinach, or Saag Goshth, is a well-known recipe from the Punjab, and a great favourite of mine. It is important to use red (bell) peppers as they add such a distinctive flavour to the dish. Serve with plain boiled rice, Naan or Paratha.

SERVES 4–6

INGREDIENTS

1 tsp ginger pulp
1 tsp garlic pulp
1½ tsp chilli powder
1 tsp salt
1 tsp garam masala
6 tbsp corn oil
2 medium onions, sliced
675 g/1½ lb lean lamb, cut into 5 cm/2 in cubes
600–900 ml/1–1½ pints/2½–3¾ cups water
400 g/14 oz fresh spinach
1 large red (bell) pepper, seeded and chopped
3 fresh green chillies, chopped
3 tbsp chopped fresh coriander (cilantro)
1 tbsp lemon juice (optional)

1 Mix together the ginger, garlic, chilli powder, salt and garam masala in a bowl. Set to one side.

2 Heat the oil in a medium saucepan. Add the onions and fry for 10–12 minutes or until well browned.

3 Add the cubed lamb to the sizzling onions and stir-fry for about 2 minutes.

4 ▲ Tip in the spice mixture and stir thoroughly until the meat pieces are well coated.

5 Pour in the water and bring to the boil. As soon as it is boiling, cover the pan and lower the heat. Cook gently for 25–35 minutes without letting the contents of the pan burn.

6 ▲ If there is still a lot of water in the pan when the meat has become tender, remove the lid and boil briskly to evaporate any excess.

7 ▲ Meanwhile, wash and chop the spinach roughly before blanching it for about 1 minute in a pan of boiling water. Drain well.

8 ▲ Add the spinach to the lamb as soon as the water has evaporated. Fry over a medium heat for 7–10 minutes, using a wooden spoon in a semi-circular motion, scraping the bottom of the pan as you stir.

9 ▲ Add the red (bell) pepper, green chillies and fresh coriander (cilantro) to the pan and stir over a medium heat for 2 minutes. Sprinkle on the lemon juice (if using) and serve immediately.

COOK'S TIP

Frozen spinach can also be used for the dish, but try to find whole leaf spinach rather than the chopped kind. Allow the frozen spinach to thaw, then drain well; there is no need to blanch it.

Kashmiri-Style Lamb

This curry originated in Kashmir, and derives its name – Rogan Josh – from the chillies originally used in the dish. The chilli powder may be reduced for a milder flavour, just add the paprika and 2 tsp tomato purée (paste) to retain the colour.

SERVES 4–6

INGREDIENTS
4 tbsp vegetable oil
1/4 tsp asafoetida
900 g/2 lb lean lamb, cubed
1 piece fresh ginger, 5 cm/2 in long, crushed
2 cloves garlic, crushed
4 tbsp rogan josh masala paste
1 tsp chilli powder or 2 tsp sweet paprika

8–10 strands saffron (optional), plus more for garnishing
salt, to taste
about 150 ml/1/4 pint/2/3 cup natural (plain) yogurt, beaten

1 ▲ Heat the oil in a pan and fry the asafoetida and lamb, stirring well to seal the meat. Reduce the heat, cover and cook for about 10 minutes.

2 Add all the remaining ingredients except the yogurt and almonds and mix well. If the meat is too dry, add a very small quantity of boiling water. Cover the pan and cook on a low heat for a further 10 minutes.

3 ▲ Remove the pan from the heat and leave to cool a little. Add the yogurt, 1 tbsp at a time, stirring constantly to avoid curdling. Return to a low heat and cook uncovered until thick. Garnish with a spoonful of yogurt and a few saffron strands.

Hot Dry Meat Curry

This dish is nearly as hot as Phaal (India's hottest curry) but the spices can still be distinguished above the chilli.

SERVES 4–6

INGREDIENTS
2 tbsp vegetable oil
1 large onion, finely sliced
1 piece fresh ginger, 5 cm/2 in long, crushed
4 cloves garlic, crushed
6–8 curry leaves
3 tbsp extra hot curry paste
3 tsp chilli powder
1 tsp five-spice powder
1 tsp turmeric
salt, to taste
900 g/2 lb lean lamb, beef or pork, cubed
175 ml/6 fl oz/3/4 cup thick coconut milk
chopped tomato and coriander (cilantro) leaves, to garnish

1 Heat the oil in a large saucepan and fry the sliced onion, ginger, garlic and curry leaves until the onion is soft, stirring occasionally. Stir in the curry paste, chilli, five-spice powder, turmeric and salt and cook for a few moments, stirring frequently.

2 ▲ Add the meat and stir well over a medium heat to seal and evenly brown the meat pieces. Keep stirring until the oil separates. Cover and cook for about 20 minutes.

3 ▲ Add the coconut milk, mix well and simmer until the meat is cooked. Towards the end of cooking, uncover the pan to reduce the excess liquid. Garnish and serve hot.

Kashmiri-Style Lamb (top) and Hot Dry Meat Curry

Spicy Lamb Tikka

One of the best ways of tenderizing meat is to marinate it in papaya, which must be unripe or it will lend its sweetness to what should be a savory dish. Papaya, or paw-paw, is readily available from most large supermarkets.

SERVES 4

INGREDIENTS
675 g/1½ lb lean lamb, cubed
1 unripe papaya
3 tbsp natural (plain) yogurt
1 tsp ginger pulp
1 tsp chilli powder
1 tsp garlic pulp
¼ tsp turmeric
2 tsp ground coriander
1 tsp ground cumin
1 tsp salt
2 tbsp lemon juice
1 tbsp chopped fresh coriander (cilantro), plus extra to garnish
¼ tsp red food colouring
300 ml/½ pint/1¼ cups corn oil
lemon wedges
onion rings

I ▲ Place the lamb in a large mixing bowl. Peel the papaya, cut in half and scoop out the seeds. Cut the flesh into cubes and blend in a food processor or blender until it is pulped, adding about 1 tbsp water if necessary.

2 ▲ Pour 2 tbsp of the papaya pulp over the lamb cubes and rub it in well with your fingers. Set to one side for at least 3 hours.

3 ▲ Meanwhile, mix together the yogurt, ginger, chilli powder, garlic, turmeric, ground coriander, ground cumin, salt, lemon juice, fresh coriander (cilantro), red food colouring and 2 tbsp of the oil, and set to one side.

4 ▲ Pour the spicy yogurt mixture over the lamb and mix together well.

5 ▲ Heat the remaining oil in a deep round-bottomed frying pan (skillet) or a karahi. Lower the heat slightly and add the lamb cubes, a few at a time.

6 Deep-fry each batch for 5–7 minutes or until the lamb is thoroughly cooked and tender. Keep the cooked pieces warm while the remainder is fried.

7 Transfer to a serving dish and garnish with lemon wedges, onion rings and fresh coriander. Serve with Raita and freshly baked Naan.

COOK'S TIP

A good-quality meat tenderizer, available from supermarkets, can be used in place of the papaya. However, the meat will need a longer marinating time and should ideally be left to tenderize overnight.

Lamb with Peas and Mint

A simple minced (ground) lamb dish, this is easy to prepare and very versatile. It is equally delicious whether served with plain boiled rice or Wholemeal (Whole-Wheat) Chapatis.

SERVES 4

INGREDIENTS
2 tbsp corn oil
1 medium onion, chopped
½ tsp garlic pulp
½ tsp ginger pulp
½ tsp chilli powder
¼ tsp turmeric
1 tsp ground coriander
1 tsp salt
2 medium tomatoes, sliced
275 g/10 oz lean leg of lamb, minced
    (ground)
1 large carrot, sliced or cut into batons
75 g/3 oz/½ cup petit pois
1 tbsp chopped fresh mint
1 tbsp chopped fresh coriander (cilantro)
1 fresh green chilli, chopped
coriander (cilantro) sprigs

NUTRITIONAL VALUES (per portion)	
Total fat	12.37 g
Saturated fat	3.83 g
Cholesterol	55.89 mg
Energy (kcals/kj)	210/882

1 ▲ In a medium saucepan or a deep frying pan (skillet), heat the oil and fry the chopped onions over a medium heat for 5 minutes until golden.

2 ▲ Meanwhile, in a small mixing bowl, blend together the garlic, ginger, chilli powder, turmeric, ground coriander and salt.

3 ▲ When the onions are ready, add the sliced tomatoes and the spice mixture and stir-fry for about 2 minutes.

4 ▲ Add the minced (ground) lamb to the mixture and stir-fry for about 7–10 minutes.

5 ▲ Break up any lumps of meat which may form, using a potato masher if necessary.

6 Finally add the carrot, petit pois, fresh mint, coriander (cilantro) and the fresh green chilli and mix all these together well.

7 Stir-fry for another 2–3 minutes and serve hot, garnished with the coriander sprigs.

Khara Masala Lamb

Whole spices (khara) are used in this curry so you should warn the diners of their presence! Delicious served with freshly baked Naan or a rice accompaniment, this dish is best made with good-quality spring lamb.

SERVES 4

INGREDIENTS

5 tbsp corn oil
2 medium onions, chopped
1 tsp shredded ginger
1 tsp sliced garlic
6 whole dried red chillies
3 cardamom pods
2 cinnamon sticks
6 black peppercorns
3 cloves
1/2 tsp salt
450 g/1 lb boned leg of lamb, cubed
600 ml/1 pint/2 1/2 cups water
2 fresh green chillies, sliced
2 tbsp chopped fresh coriander (cilantro)

1 Heat the oil in a large saucepan. Lower the heat slightly and fry the onions until they are lightly browned.

2 ▲ Add half the ginger and half the garlic and stir well.

3 ▲ Throw in half the red chillies, the cardamoms, cinnamon, peppercorns, cloves and salt.

4 ▲ Add the lamb and fry over a medium heat. Stir continuously with a semi-circular movement, using a wooden spoon to scrape the bottom of the pan. Continue in this way for about 5 minutes.

5 Pour in the water, cover with a lid and cook over a medium-low heat for 35–40 minutes, or until the water has evaporated and the meat is tender.

6 ▲ Add the rest of the ginger, garlic and dried red chillies, along with the fresh green chillies and fresh coriander (cilantro).

7 ▲ Continue to stir over the heat until you see some free oil on the sides of the pan. Transfer to a serving dish and serve immediately.

COOK'S TIP

The action of stirring the meat and spices together using a semi-circular motion, as described in step 4, is called bhoono-ing. It ensures that the meat becomes well-coated and combined with the spice mixture before the cooking liquid is added.

Spicy Meat Loaf

This mixture is baked in the oven and provides a hearty meal on cold winter days.

SERVES 4–6

INGREDIENTS
*5 eggs
450 g/1 lb lean minced (ground) beef
2 tbsp ginger pulp
2 tbsp garlic pulp
6 fresh green chillies, chopped
2 small onions, finely chopped
½ tsp turmeric
50 g/2 oz/2 cups fresh coriander, chopped
175 g/6 oz potato, grated
salt, to taste
salad leaves, to serve
lemon twist, to garnish*

1 ▲ Preheat the oven to 180°C/350°F/Gas 4. Beat 2 eggs until fluffy and pour into a greased baking tray.

2 Knead together the meat, ginger and garlic, 4 green chillies, 1 chopped onion, 1 beaten egg, the turmeric, fresh coriander, potato and salt. Pack into the baking tray and smooth the surface. Cook in the preheated oven for 45 minutes.

3 ▲ Beat the remaining eggs and fold in the remaining green chillies and onion. Remove the baking tray from the oven and pour the mixture all over the meat. Return to the oven and cook until the eggs have set. Serve hot on on a bed of salad leaves, garnished with a twist of lemon.

Koftas

Serve these tasty kebabs piping hot with Naan, Raita and Tomato Salad. Leftover kebabs can be coarsely chopped and packed into pitta bread spread with Fresh Coriander (Cilantro) Relish to serve as a quick snack.

MAKES 20–25

INGREDIENTS
*450 g/1 lb lean minced (ground) beef or lamb
2 tbsp ginger pulp
2 tbsp garlic pulp
4 fresh green chillies, finely chopped
1 small onion, finely chopped
1 egg
½ tsp turmeric
1 tsp garam masala
50 g/2 oz/2 cups fresh coriander (cilantro), chopped
4–6 fresh mint leaves, chopped, or ½ tsp mint sauce*

*175 g/6 oz raw potato
salt, to taste
vegetable oil, for deep-frying*

2 Shape the mixture into portions the size of golf balls. Set aside on a plate and leave the koftas to rest for about 25 minutes.

1 ▲ Place the first 10 ingredients in a large bowl. Grate the potato into the bowl, and season with salt. Knead together to blend well and form a soft dough.

3 ▲ In a karahi or frying pan (skillet), heat the oil to medium-hot and fry the koftas in small batches until they are golden brown in colour. Drain well and serve hot.

Spicy Meat Loaf (top) and Koftas

Balti Minced (Ground) Lamb Koftas with Vegetables

These koftas look most attractive served on their bed of vegetables, especially if you make them quite small.

SERVES 4

INGREDIENTS
Koftas
450 g/1 lb lean minced (ground) lamb
1 tsp garam masala
1 tsp ground cumin
1 tsp ground coriander
1 tsp garlic pulp
1 tsp chilli powder
1 tsp salt
1 tbsp chopped fresh coriander (cilantro)
1 small onion, finely diced
150 ml/¼ pint/⅔ cup corn oil

Vegetables
3 tbsp corn oil
1 bunch spring onions (scallions), roughly chopped
½ large red (bell) pepper, seeded and chopped
½ large green (bell) pepper, seeded and chopped
175 g/6 oz/1 cup sweetcorn (corn kernels)
225 g/8 oz/1½ cups canned butter beans, drained
½ small cauliflower, cut into florets (flowerets)
4 fresh green chillies, chopped

1 tsp chopped fresh mint
1 tbsp chopped fresh coriander (cilantro)
1 tbsp shredded ginger
lime slices
1 tbsp lemon juice

I Put the minced (ground) lamb into a food processor or blender and process for about 1 minute.

2 ▲ Transfer the lamb into a medium bowl. Add the garam masala, ground cumin, ground coriander, garlic, chilli powder, salt, fresh coriander (cilantro) and onion, and use your fingers to blend everything thoroughly.

3 Cover the bowl and set aside in the refrigerator.

4 ▲ Heat the oil for the vegetables in a deep round-bottomed frying pan (skillet) or a medium karahi. Add the spring onions (scallions) and stir-fry for about 2 minutes.

5 ▲ Add the (bell) peppers, sweetcorn (corn kernels), butter beans, cauliflower and green chillies, and stir-fry over a high heat for about 2 minutes. Set to one side.

6 ▲ Using your hands, roll small pieces of the kofta mixture into golf-ball sized portions. It should make between 12 and 16 koftas.

7 ▲ Heat the oil for the koftas in a frying pan. Lower the heat slightly and add the koftas, a few at a time. Shallow-fry each batch, turning the koftas, until they are evenly browned.

8 Remove from the oil with a slotted spoon, and drain on kitchen paper (paper towels).

9 ▲ Put the vegetable mixture back over a medium heat, and add the cooked koftas. Stir the mixture gently for about 5 minutes, or until everything is heated through.

10 Garnish with the mint, coriander, shredded ginger and lime slices. Just before serving, sprinkle over the lemon juice.

Spicy Spring Lamb Roast

LOW-FAT RECIPE

There are a number of ways of roasting lamb and several different spice mixtures which people use. This is one of my favourite variations.

SERVES 6

INGREDIENTS
1.5 kg/3 lb leg spring lamb
1 tsp chilli powder
1 tsp garlic pulp
1 tsp ground coriander
1 tsp ground cumin
1 tsp salt
2 tsp desiccated (shredded) coconut
2 tsp ground almonds
3 tbsp natural (plain) low-fat yogurt
2 tbsp lemon juice
2 tbsp sultanas (golden raisins)
2 tbsp corn oil

Garnish
mixed salad leaves
fresh coriander (cilantro) sprigs
2 tomatoes, quartered
1 large carrot, cut into julienne strips
lemon wedges

NUTRITIONAL VALUES (per portion)	
Total fat	11.96 g
Saturated fat	4.70 g
Cholesterol	67.38 mg
Energy (kcals/kj)	197/825

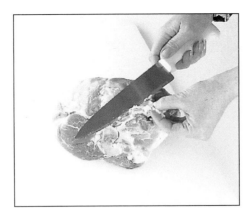

I ▲ Preheat the oven to 180°C/350°F/ Gas 4. Trim off the fat, rinse and pat dry the leg of lamb and set aside on a sheet of foil large enough to enclose the whole joint.

2 ▲ In a medium bowl, mix together the chilli powder, garlic, ground coriander, ground cumin and salt.

3 ▲ Grind together in a food processor the desiccated (shredded) coconut, ground almonds, yogurt, lemon juice and sultanas (golden raisins).

4 ▲ Add the contents of the food processor to the spice mixture together with the corn oil and mix together. Pour this onto the leg of lamb and rub over the meat.

5 Enclose the meat in the foil and place in an ovenproof dish. Cook in the preheated oven for about 1½ hours.

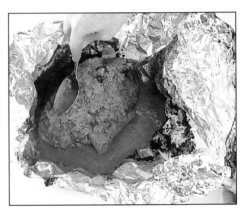

6 ▲ Remove the lamb from the oven, open the foil and using the back of a spoon spread the mixture evenly over the meat. Return the lamb, uncovered, to the oven for another 45 minutes or until it is cooked right through and is tender.

7 Slice the meat and serve with the garnish ingredients.

COOK'S TIP

If you don't have any ready-ground almonds to hand, simply process flaked (slivered) or whole blanched almonds in a food processor or coffee grinder.

Lamb Chops Kashmiri-Style

These chops are cooked in a unique way, being first boiled in milk, and then fried. Despite the large number of spices used in this recipe, the actual dish has a mild flavour, and is delicious served with fried rice and a lentil dish.

SERVES 4

INGREDIENTS
8–12 lamb chops, about 50–75 g/2–3 oz
each
1 piece cinnamon bark
1 bay leaf
¹/₂ tsp fennel seeds
¹/₂ tsp black peppercorns
3 green cardamom pods
1 tsp salt
600 ml/1 pint/2¹/₂ cups milk
150 ml/¹/₄ pint/²/₃ cup evaporated milk
150 ml/¹/₄ pint/²/₃ cup natural (plain)
yogurt
2 tbsp plain (all-purpose) flour
1 tsp chilli powder
1 tsp ginger pulp
¹/₂ tsp garam masala
¹/₂ tsp garlic pulp
pinch of salt
300 ml/¹/₂ pint/1¹/₄ cups corn oil
mint sprigs
lime quarters

I ▲ Trim the lamb chops and place them in a large saucepan with the cinnamon bark, bay leaf, fennel seeds, peppercorns, cardamoms, salt and milk. Bring to the boil over a high heat.

2 ▲ Lower the heat and cook for 12–15 minutes, or until the milk has reduced to about half its original volume. At this stage, add the evaporated milk and lower the heat further. Simmer until the chops are cooked through and the milk has evaporated.

3 ▲ While the chops are cooking, blend together the yogurt, flour, chilli powder, ginger, garam masala, garlic and a pinch of salt in a mixing bowl.

4 ▲ Remove the chops from the saucepan and discard the whole spices. Add the chops to the spicy yogurt mixture.

5 ▲ Heat the oil in a deep round-bottomed frying pan (skillet) or medium karahi. Lower the heat slightly and add the chops. Fry until they are golden brown, turning them once or twice as they cook.

6 Transfer to a serving dish, and garnish with mint sprigs and lime quarters.

COOK'S TIP

These delicious lamb chops, with their crunchy yogurt coating, make ideal finger food to serve at a buffet or drinks party.

Mince Kebabs

Serve this Indian hamburger in a bun with chilli sauce and salad or unaccompanied as an appetizer.

SERVES 4–6

INGREDIENTS
2 onions, finely chopped
250 g/9 oz lean lamb, cut into small cubes
50 g/2 oz bengal gram
1 tsp cumin seeds
1 tsp garam masala
4–6 fresh green chillies
*1 piece fresh ginger, 5 cm/2 in long,
    crushed*
salt, to taste
175 ml/6 fl oz/³/4 cup water

*few fresh coriander (cilantro) and mint
    leaves, chopped*
juice of 1 lemon
1 tbsp gram flour (besan)
2 eggs, beaten
vegetable oil, for shallow-frying
¹/2 lime

1 Put the first 8 ingredients and the water into a pan and bring to the boil. Simmer, covered, until the meat and dhal are cooked.

2 Remove the lid and cook uncovered to reduce the excess liquid. Cool, and grind to a paste.

3 ▲ Place the mixture in a mixing bowl and add the fresh coriander (cilantro) and mint, lemon juice and flour. Knead well. Divide into 10–12 portions and roll each into a ball, then flatten slightly. Chill for 1 hour. Dip the kebabs in the beaten egg and shallow-fry each side until golden brown. Serve hot with the lime.

Portuguese Pork

This dish displays the influence of Portuguese cooking on Indian cuisine.

SERVES 4–6

INGREDIENTS

115 g/4 oz deep-fried onions, crushed
4 red chillies, or 1 tsp chilli powder
4 tbsp vindaloo masala paste
6 tbsp white wine vinegar
6 tbsp tomato purée (paste)
1/2 tsp fenugreek seeds
1 tsp turmeric
*1 tsp crushed mustard seeds, or 1/2 tsp
    mustard powder*
salt, to taste
1 1/2 tsp sugar
900 g/2 lb boneless pork spareribs, cubed
250 ml/8 fl oz/1 cup water
plain boiled rice, to serve

1 ▲ Place all the ingredients except the water and rice in a heavy steel pan and mix well. Marinate for about 2 hours.

2 ▲ Transfer to a frying pan (skillet), add the water and mix well. Bring to the boil and simmer gently for about 2 hours. Adjust the seasoning. Serve hot with the plain boiled rice.

Balti Mini Lamb Kebabs (Kabobs) with Baby Onions

This is rather an unusual Balti dish as the kebabs (kabobs) are first grilled (broiled) before being added to the karahi for the final stage of cooking.

SERVES 6

INGREDIENTS
450 g/1 lb lean minced (ground) lamb
1 medium onion, finely chopped
1 tsp garam masala
1 tsp garlic pulp
2 medium fresh green chillies, finely chopped
2 tbsp chopped fresh coriander (cilantro)
1 tsp salt
1 tbsp plain (all-purpose) flour
4 tbsp corn oil
12 baby onions
4 fresh green chillies, sliced
12 cherry tomatoes
2 tbsp chopped fresh coriander

1 ▲ Blend together the minced (ground) lamb, onion, garam masala, garlic, green chillies, fresh coriander (cilantro), salt and flour in a medium bowl. Use your hands to make sure that all the ingredients are thoroughly mixed together.

2 Transfer the mixture to a food processor and process for about 1 minute, to make the mixture even finer in texture.

3 ▲ Put the mixture back into the bowl. Break off small pieces, about the size of a lime, and wrap them around skewers to form small sausage shapes. Put about 2 kebabs (kabobs) on each skewer.

4 ▲ Once you have used up all the mixture, baste the kebabs with 1 tbsp of the oil and place under a preheated hot grill (broiler) for 12–15 minutes, turning and basting occasionally, until they are evenly browned.

5 ▲ Heat the remaining 3 tbsp of the oil in a deep round-bottomed frying pan (skillet) or a medium karahi. Lower the heat slightly and add the whole baby onions. As soon as they start to darken, add the fresh chillies and tomatoes.

6 ▲ Remove the mini kebabs from their skewers and add them to the onion and tomato mixture. Stir gently for about 3 minutes to heat them through.

7 Transfer to a serving dish and garnish with fresh coriander. Serve with Spicy Balti Potatoes and Paratha.

Stuffed Aubergines (Eggplants) with Lamb

LOW-FAT RECIPE

Minced (ground) lamb and aubergines (eggplants) go really well together. This is an attractive dish, using different coloured (bell) peppers in the lightly spiced stuffing mixture.

SERVES 4

INGREDIENTS

2 medium aubergines (eggplants)
2 tbsp vegetable oil
1 medium onion, sliced
1 tsp ginger pulp
1 tsp chilli powder
1 tsp garlic pulp
1/4 tsp turmeric
1 tsp salt
1 tsp ground coriander
1 medium tomato, chopped
350 g/12 oz lean leg of lamb, minced (ground)
1 medium green (bell) pepper, roughly chopped
1 medium orange (bell) pepper, roughly chopped
2 tbsp chopped fresh coriander (cilantro)

Garnish

1/2 onion, sliced
2 cherry tomatoes, quartered
fresh coriander (cilantro) sprigs

NUTRITIONAL VALUES (per portion)	
Total fat	13.92 g
Saturated fat	4.36 g
Cholesterol	67.15 mg
Energy (kcals/kj)	239/1003

2 In a medium saucepan, heat 1 tbsp oil and fry the sliced onion until golden brown.

3 ▲ Gradually stir in the ginger, chilli powder, garlic, turmeric, salt and ground coriander. Add the chopped tomato, lower the heat and stir-fry for about 5 minutes.

4 ▲ Add the minced (ground) lamb and continue to stir-fry over a medium heat for 7–10 minutes.

5 ▲ Add the chopped (bell) peppers and fresh coriander (cilantro) to the lamb mixture and stir well.

6 ▲ Spoon the lamb mixture into the aubergine shells and brush the edge of the shells with the remaining oil. Bake in the preheated oven for 20–25 minutes until cooked through and browned on top.

7 Serve with the garnish ingredients and either a green salad or plain boiled rice.

VARIATION

For a special occasion, stuffed baby aubergines (eggplants) look particularly attractive. Use 4 small aubergines, leaving the stalks intact, and prepare and cook as described above. Reduce the baking time slightly, if necessary. Large tomatoes or courgettes also make an excellent alternative to aubergines.

1 Preheat the oven to 180°C/350°F/ Gas 4. Cut the aubergines (eggplants) in half lengthways and scoop out most of the flesh and discard. Place the aubergine shells in a lightly greased ovenproof dish.

Beef Madras

This popular South Indian curry is mainly prepared by Muslims and is traditionally made with beef.

SERVES 4–6

INGREDIENTS
4 tbsp vegetable oil
1 large onion, finely sliced
3–4 cloves
4 green cardamom pods
2 whole star anise
4 fresh green chillies, chopped
2 red chillies, chopped (fresh or dried)
3 tbsp Madras masala paste
1 tsp turmeric
450 g/1 lb lean beef, cubed
4 tbsp tamarind juice
salt, to taste

sugar, to taste
fresh coriander (cilantro) sprigs, to garnish

1 ▲ Heat the oil in a pan and fry the onion until it is golden brown. Lower the heat and add all the spice ingredients and fry for a further 2–3 minutes.

2 Add the beef to the pan and mix well. Cover and cook on a low heat until the beef is tender. Remove the lid from the pan and cook uncovered on a higher heat for the last few minutes to reduce any excess liquid.

3 ▲ Fold in the tamarind juice, salt and sugar. Reheat the dish and serve hot, garnished with the fresh coriander (cilantro) sprigs.

Lamb Korma

This is a creamy, aromatic dish with no 'hot' taste. It comes from the kitchens of the Nizam of Hyderabad.

SERVES 4–6

INGREDIENTS
1 tbsp white sesame seeds
1 tbsp white poppy seeds
50 g/2 oz blanched almonds
2 fresh green chillies, seeded
6 cloves garlic, sliced
1 piece fresh ginger, 5 cm/2 in long, sliced
1 onion, finely chopped
3 tbsp ghee or vegetable oil
6 green cardamom pods
1 piece cinnamon stick, 5 cm/2 in long
4 cloves
900 g/2 lb lean lamb, cubed
1 tsp ground cumin
1 tsp ground coriander
salt, to taste

300 ml/½ pint/1¼ cups double (heavy) cream mixed with ½ tsp cornflour (cornstarch)
roasted sesame seeds, to garnish

1 ▲ Heat a frying pan (skillet) without any liquid and dry-roast the first 7 ingredients. Cool the mixture and grind to a fine paste using a pestle and mortar or food processor. Heat the ghee or oil in a frying pan.

2 Fry the cardamom pods, cinnamon and cloves over a medium heat until the cloves swell. Add the lamb, ground cumin and coriander and the prepared paste, and season. Cover the pan and cook until the lamb is almost done, stirring occasionally.

3 ▲ Remove from the heat, cool a little and gradually fold in the cream, reserving 1 tsp to garnish. To serve, gently reheat the lamb uncovered and serve hot, garnished with the sesame seeds and the remaining cream.

Balti Stuffed Vegetables

Aubergines (eggplants) and (bell) peppers make an excellent combination. Here they are stuffed with an aromatic lamb filling and served on a bed of sautéed onions.

SERVES 6

INGREDIENTS
3 small aubergines (eggplants)
1 each red, green and yellow (bell) peppers

Stuffing
3 tbsp corn oil
3 medium onions, sliced
1 tsp chilli powder
¹/₄ tsp turmeric
1 tsp ground coriander
1 tsp ground cumin
1 tsp ginger pulp
1 tsp garlic pulp
1 tsp salt
450 g/1 lb lean minced (ground) lamb
3 fresh green chillies, chopped
2 tbsp chopped fresh coriander (cilantro)

Sautéed onions
3 tbsp corn oil
1 tsp mixed onion, mustard, fenugreek and white cumin seeds
4 dried red chillies
3 medium onions, roughly chopped
1 tsp salt
1 tsp chilli powder
2 medium tomatoes, sliced
2 fresh green chillies, chopped
2 tbsp chopped fresh coriander

1 Prepare the vegetables. Slit the aubergines (eggplants) lengthways up to the stalks; keep the stalks intact. Cut the tops off the (bell) peppers and remove the seeds. You can retain the pepper tops and use them as 'lids' once the vegetables have been stuffed, if wished.

2 Make the stuffing. Heat the oil in a medium saucepan. Add the onions and fry for about 3 minutes. Lower the heat and add the chilli powder, turmeric, ground coriander, ground cumin, ginger, garlic and salt, and stir-fry for about 1 minute. Add the minced (ground) lamb to the pan and turn up the heat.

3 ▲ Stir-fry for 7–10 minutes or until the mince is cooked, using a wooden spoon to scrape the bottom of the pan. Throw in the green chillies and fresh coriander (cilantro) towards the end. Remove from the heat, cover and set to one side.

4 Make the sautéed onions. Heat the oil in a deep round-bottomed frying pan (skillet) or a karahi and throw in the mixed onion, mustard, fenugreek and white cumin seeds together with the dried red chillies, and fry for about 1 minute. Add the onions and fry for about 2 minutes or until soft.

5 Add the salt, chilli powder, tomatoes, green chillies and fresh coriander. Cook for a further minute. Remove from the heat and set to one side.

6 ▲ The minced lamb should by now be cool enough to stuff the prepared aubergines and peppers. Fill the vegetables quite loosely with the meat mixture.

7 ▲ As you stuff the vegetables, place them on top of the sautéed onions in the karahi. Cover with foil, making sure the foil doesn't touch the food, and cook over a low heat for about 15 minutes.

8 The dish is ready as soon as the aubergines and peppers are tender. Serve with a dish of plain boiled rice or Colourful Pullao Rice.

VARIATION

Large beef tomatoes are also delicious stuffed with the lightly spiced lamb mixture. Simply cut off the tops and scoop out the cores, seeds and some of the pulp and cook as described above.

Beef with Green Beans

LOW-FAT RECIPE

Green beans cooked with beef is a variation on the traditional recipe using lamb. The sliced red (bell) pepper used here makes this dish colourful as well as delicious.

SERVES 4

INGREDIENTS

275 g/10 oz fine green beans, cut into 2.5
    cm/1 in pieces
2 tbsp vegetable oil
1 medium onion, sliced
1 tsp ginger pulp
1 tsp garlic pulp
1 tsp chilli powder
1¼ tsp salt
¼ tsp turmeric
2 tomatoes, chopped
450 g/1 lb beef, cubed
1.2 litres/2 pints/5 cups water
1 tbsp chopped fresh coriander (cilantro)
1 red (bell) pepper, sliced
2 fresh green chillies, chopped

NUTRITIONAL VALUES (per portion)	
Total fat	11.60 g
Saturated fat	2.89 g
Cholesterol	66.96 mg
Energy (kcals/kj)	241/1011

1 ▲ Boil the green beans in salted water for about 5 minutes, then drain and set aside.

2 ▲ Heat the oil in a large saucepan and fry the sliced onion until it turns golden brown.

3 ▲ Mix together the ginger, garlic, chilli powder, salt, turmeric and chopped tomatoes. Spoon this mixture into the onions and stir-fry for 5–7 minutes.

4 Add the beef and stir-fry for a further 3 minutes. Pour in the water, bring to a boil and lower the heat. Cover and cook for 45 minutes to 1 hour until most of the water has evaporated and the meat is tender.

5 ▲ Add the green beans and mix everything together well.

6 ▲ Finally, add the red (bell) pepper, fresh coriander (cilantro) and chopped green chillies and cook, stirring, for a further 7–10 minutes.

7 Serve hot with Wholemeal (Whole-Wheat) Chapatis.

COOK'S TIP

Frying onions in very little oil requires some patience. They will take a little longer to brown and should be stirred only occasionally. Excessive stirring will draw the moisture out of the onions and make them even more difficult to fry.

Steak and Kidney with Spinach

When this dish is cooked in India, the spinach is often pulverized. Here, it is coarsely chopped and added in the last stages of cooking, which retains the nutritional value of the spinach and gives the dish a lovely appearance.

SERVES 4–6

INGREDIENTS
2 tbsp vegetable oil
1 large onion, finely chopped
1 piece fresh ginger, 5 cm/2 in long, crushed
4 cloves garlic, crushed
4 tbsp mild curry paste, or 4 tbsp mild curry powder
¼ tsp turmeric
salt, to taste
900 g/2 lb steak and kidney, cubed
450 g/1 lb fresh spinach, trimmed, washed and chopped or 450 g/1 lb frozen spinach, thawed and drained
4 tbsp tomato purée (paste)
2 large tomatoes, finely chopped

1 ▲ Heat the oil in a frying pan (skillet) and fry the onion, ginger and garlic until the onion is soft and the ginger and garlic turn golden brown.

3 ▲ Add the spinach and tomato purée (paste) and mix well. Cook uncovered until the spinach is softened and most of the liquid evaporated.

2 ▲ Lower the heat and add the curry paste or powder, turmeric, salt and meat and mix well. Cover and cook until the meat is just tender.

4 ▲ Fold in the chopped tomatoes. Increase the heat and cook for about 5 minutes.

Lentils with Lamb and Tomatoes

This dish is full of protein and has a deliciously light texture. Serve with Colourful Pullao Rice.

SERVES 4

INGREDIENTS
4 tbsp corn oil
1 bay leaf
2 cloves
4 black peppercorns
1 medium onion, sliced
450 g/1 lb lean lamb, boned and cubed
¼ tsp turmeric
1½ tsp chilli powder
1 tsp crushed coriander seeds
2.5 cm/1 in cinnamon stick
1 tsp garlic pulp
1½ tsp salt
1.5 litres/2½ pints/6¼ cups water
50 g/2 oz/⅓ cup round yellow lentils (chana dhal), or yellow split peas
2 medium tomatoes, quartered
2 fresh green chillies, chopped
1 tbsp chopped fresh coriander (cilantro)

I ▲ Heat the oil in a deep round-bottomed frying pan (skillet) or a karahi. Lower the heat slightly and add the bay leaf, cloves, peppercorns and onion. Fry for about 5 minutes, or until the onions are golden brown.

2 ▲ Add the cubed lamb, turmeric, chilli powder, coriander seeds, cinnamon stick, garlic and most of the salt, and stir-fry for about 5 minutes over a medium heat.

3 Pour in 900 ml/1½ pints/3¾ cups of the water and cover the pan with a lid or foil, making sure the foil does not come into contact with the food. Simmer over a low heat for about 35–40 minutes, or until the water has evaporated and the lamb is tender.

4 Put the lentils into a saucepan with 600 ml/1 pint/2½ cups water and boil for about 12–15 minutes, or until the water has almost evaporated and the lentils are soft enough to be easily mashed. If the lentils are too thick, add up to 150 ml/¼ pint/⅔ cup water to loosen them.

5 ▲ When the lamb is tender, stir-fry the mixture using a wooden spoon, until some free oil begins to appear on the sides of the pan.

6 ▲ Add the cooked lentils to the lamb and mix together well.

7 ▲ Add the tomatoes, chillies and fresh coriander (cilantro) and serve.

COOK'S TIP

Boned and cubed chicken can be used in place of the lamb. At step 3, reduce the amount of water to 300 ml/½ pint/1¼ cups and cook uncovered, stirring occasionally, for 10–15 minutes or until the water has evaporated and the chicken is cooked through.

Hot-and-Sour Meat and Lentil Curry

Dhansak is one of the best-known Parsi dishes and is a favourite for Sunday lunch. This dish has a hot, sweet-and-sour flavour, through which should rise the slightly bitter flavour of fenugreek.

SERVES 4–6

INGREDIENTS

6 tbsp vegetable oil
5 fresh green chillies, chopped
1 piece fresh ginger, 2.5 cm/1 in long, crushed
3 cloves garlic crushed
2 bay leaves
1 piece cinnamon stick, 5 cm/2 in long
900 g/2 lb lean lamb, cubed
600 ml/1 pint/2½ cups water
175 g/6 oz/⅔ cup red gram
50 g/2 oz/¼ cup each bengal gram, small split yellow lentils (moong dhal) and split red lentils (masoor dhal)
2 potatoes, cubed and soaked in water
1 aubergine (eggplant), cubed and soaked in water
4 onions, finely sliced, deep-fried and drained
50 g/2 oz fresh spinach, trimmed, washed and chopped or 50 g/2 oz frozen spinach, thawed and drained
25 g/1 oz fenugreek leaves, fresh or dried
115 g/4 oz carrots or pumpkin, cubed
115 g/4 oz/4 cups fresh coriander (cilantro), chopped
50 g/2 oz fresh mint, chopped, or 1 tbsp mint sauce
2 tbsp dhansak masala
2 tbsp sambhar masala
salt, to taste
2 tsp brown sugar
4 tbsp tamarind juice
1 clove garlic, sliced

COOK'S TIP

Chicken or prawns (shrimp) can be used instead of the lamb. If using chicken, reduce the cooking time so that the meat does not become shredded or stringy; if you are using prawns, cook only until the tails turn bright orange/pink in colour.

1 ▲ Heat 3 tbsp of the oil in a saucepan or deep frying pan (skillet) and fry the green chillies, ginger and crushed garlic cloves for 2 minutes. Add the bay leaves, cinnamon, lamb and water. Bring to the boil then simmer until the lamb is half cooked.

2 ▲ Drain the water into another pan and put the lamb aside. Add the lentils to the water and cook until they are tender. Mash the lentils with the back of a spoon.

3 ▲ Drain the potatoes and aubergine (eggplant) and add to the lentils with 3 of the deep-fried onions, the spinach, fenugreek and carrot or pumpkin. Add some hot water if the mixture is too thick. Cook until the vegetables are tender, then mash again with a spoon, keeping the vegetables a little coarse.

4 ▲ Heat 1 tbsp of the oil in a frying pan (skillet) and gently fry the fresh coriander (cilantro) and mint (saving a little to garnish) with the dhansak and sambhar masala, salt and sugar. Add the lamb and fry gently for about 5 minutes.

5 ▲ Return the lamb and spices to the lentil and vegetable mixture and stir well. As lentils absorb fluids, adjust the consistency if necessary. Heat gently until the lamb is fully cooked.

6 ▲ Add the tamarind juice and mix well. Heat the remaining oil and fry the sliced clove of garlic until golden brown. Pour over the dhansak. Garnish with the remaining deep-fried onion and the reserved coriander and mint. Serve hot.

Fish & Seafood Dishes

Fish and shellfish have a surprising affinity with spices, either fairly fiery mixtures as in Balti Prawns in Hot Sauce, or as part of a blend of other aromatic ingredients, such as lime, coriander, coconut and chillies. These are used to great effect in Balti Fish Fillets in Spicy Coconut Sauce. Even just a light spicing works, too — Fish and Vegetable Kebabs make a tasty lunch dish.

Balti Fried Fish

As a child in Pakistan, I used to hear fishmongers calling out the contents of their day's catch from stalls on wheels. Nowadays, seafood is readily available in the many fish markets.

SERVES 4–6

INGREDIENTS
675 g/1½ lb cod, or any other firm,
  white fish
1 medium onion, sliced
1 tbsp lemon juice
1 tsp salt
1 tsp garlic pulp
1 tsp crushed dried red chillies
1½ tsp garam masala
2 tbsp chopped fresh coriander (cilantro)
2 medium tomatoes
2 tbsp cornflour (cornstarch)
150 ml/¼ pint/⅔ cup corn oil

I   Skin the fish and cut into small cubes. Put into the refrigerator to chill.

2 ▲ Put the onion into a bowl and add the lemon juice, salt, garlic, crushed red chillies, garam masala and fresh coriander (cilantro). Mix together well and set to one side.

3 ▲ Skin the tomatoes by dropping them into boiling water for a few seconds. Remove with a slotted spoon and gently peel off the skins. Chop the tomatoes roughly and add to the onion mixture in the bowl.

4 ▲ Place the contents of the bowl into a food processor or blender and process for about 30 seconds.

5 Remove the fish from the refrigerator. Pour the contents of the food processor or blender over the fish and mix together well.

6 ▲ Add the cornflour (cornstarch) and mix again until the fish pieces are well coated.

7 ▲ Heat the oil in a deep round-bottomed frying pan (skillet) or a karahi. Lower the heat slightly and add the fish pieces, a few at a time. Turn them gently with a slotted spoon as they will break easily. Cook for about 5 minutes until the fish is lightly browned.

8 Remove the fish pieces from the pan and drain on kitchen paper (paper towels) to absorb any excess oil. Keep warm and continue frying the remaining fish. This dish is delicious served with Apricot Chutney and Paratha.

COOK'S TIP

For busy cooks, canned tomatoes can be used instead of fresh ones – there are no skins to remove!

Prawns (Shrimp) and Fish in Herb Sauce

Bengalis are famous for their seafood dishes and always use mustard oil in recipes because it imparts a unique taste, flavour and aroma. No feast in Bengal is complete without one of these celebrated fish dishes.

SERVES 4–6

INGREDIENTS

3 cloves garlic
1 piece fresh ginger, 5 cm/2 in long
1 large leek, roughly chopped
4 fresh green chillies
1 tsp vegetable oil (optional)
4 tbsp mustard oil, or vegetable oil
1 tbsp ground coriander
1/2 tsp fennel seeds
1 tbsp crushed yellow mustard seeds, or 1 tsp mustard powder
175 ml/6 fl oz/3/4 cup thick coconut milk
225 g/8 oz huss or monkfish fillets, cut into thick chunks
225 g/8 oz fresh king prawns (jumbo shrimp), peeled and deveined with tails intact
salt, to taste
115 g/4 oz/4 cups fresh coriander (cilantro), chopped
2 fresh green chillies, to garnish

1 ▲ In a food processor, grind the garlic, ginger, leek and chillies to a coarse paste. Add a little vegetable oil if the mixture is too dry and process the mixture again.

3 ▲ Add the ground coriander, fennel seeds, mustard and coconut milk to the pan. Gently bring to the boil and then simmer, uncovered, for about 5 minutes.

2 ▲ In a frying pan (skillet), heat the mustard or vegetable oil with the paste until it is well blended. Keep the window open and take care not to overheat the mixture as any smoke from the mustard oil will sting the eyes.

4 ▲ Add the fish and simmer for 2 minutes, then fold in the prawns (shrimp) and cook until the prawns turn a bright orange/pink colour. Season with salt, fold in the fresh coriander (cilantro) and serve hot. Garnish with the fresh green chillies, if wished.

Pickled Fish Steaks

This dish is served cold, often as an appetizer. It also makes an ideal main course on a hot summer's day served with a crisp salad. Make a day or two in advance to allow the flavours to blend.

SERVES 4–6

INGREDIENTS
juice of 4 lemons
1 piece fresh ginger, 2.5 cm/1 in long, finely sliced
2 cloves garlic, finely minced
2 fresh red chillies, finely chopped
3 fresh green chillies, finely chopped
4 thick fish steaks (any firm fish)
4 tbsp vegetable oil
4–6 curry leaves
1 onion, finely chopped
1/2 tsp turmeric
1 tbsp ground coriander
150 ml/1/4 pint/2/3 cup pickling vinegar
3 tsp sugar
salt, to taste
salad leaves, to garnish
1/2 tomato, to garnish

1 ▲ In a bowl, mix the lemon juice with the ginger, garlic and chillies. Pat the fish dry and rub the mixture on all sides of the fish. Allow to marinate for 3–4 hours in the refrigerator.

2 ▲ Heat the oil in a frying pan (skillet) and fry the curry leaves, onion, turmeric and coriander until the onion is translucent.

3 ▲ Place the fish steaks in the frying pan with the marinade and cover with the onion mixture. After 5 minutes, turn the fish over gently to prevent damaging the steaks.

4 ▲ Pour in the vinegar and add the sugar and salt. Bring to the boil, then lower the heat and simmer until the fish is cooked. Carefully transfer the steaks to a large platter or individual serving dishes and pour over the vinegar mixture. Chill for 24 hours before garnishing and serving.

Fish and Vegetable Kebabs (Kabobs)

LOW-FAT RECIPE

This is a very attractive dish and served on its own will also make an excellent appetizer for eight people.

SERVES 4

INGREDIENTS

275 g/10 oz cod fillets, or any other firm,
    white fish fillets
3 tbsp lemon juice
1 tsp ginger pulp
2 fresh green chillies, very finely chopped
1 tbsp very finely chopped fresh coriander
    (cilantro)
1 tbsp very finely chopped fresh mint
1 tsp ground coriander
1 tsp salt
1 red (bell) pepper
1 green (bell) pepper
½ medium cauliflower
8–10 button mushrooms
8 cherry tomatoes
1 tbsp soya oil
1 lime, quartered

NUTRITIONAL VALUES (per portion)

Total fat	4.34 g
Saturated fat	0.51 g
Cholesterol	32.54 mg
Energy (kcals/kj)	130/546

1 ▲ Cut the fish fillets into large chunks.

2 ▲ In a large mixing bowl, blend together the lemon juice, ginger, chopped green chillies, fresh coriander (cilantro), mint, ground coriander and salt. Add the fish chunks and leave to marinate for about 30 minutes.

3 ▲ Cut the red and green (bell) peppers into large squares and divide the cauliflower into individual florets (flowerets).

4 ▲ Preheat the grill (broiler) to hot. Arrange the peppers, cauliflower florets, mushrooms and cherry tomatoes alternately with the fish pieces on 4 skewers.

5 ▲ Baste the kebabs (kabobs) with the oil and any remaining marinade. Transfer to a flameproof dish and grill (broil) under the hot grill for 7–10 minutes or until the fish is cooked right through.

6 Garnish with the lime quarters, if wished, and serve the kebabs either on their own or with Saffron and Cardamom Flavoured Rice.

VARIATION

Do use different vegetables to the ones suggested, if wished. For example, try baby corn cobs instead of mushrooms and broccoli or one of the new cultivated brassicas in place of the cauliflower.

Chunky Fish Balti with Peppers

Try to find as many different colours of (bell) peppers as possible to make this very attractive dish.

SERVES 2–4

INGREDIENTS
450 g/1 lb cod, or any other firm, white
    fish
1½ tsp ground cumin
2 tsp mango powder
1 tsp ground coriander
½ tsp chilli powder
1 tsp salt
1 tsp ginger pulp
3 tbsp cornflour (cornstarch)
150 ml/¼ pint/⅔ cup corn oil
1 each green, orange and red (bell)
    peppers, seeded and chopped
8–10 cherry tomatoes

1 ▲ Skin the fish and cut into small cubes. Put the cubes into a large mixing bowl and add the ground cumin, mango powder, ground coriander, chilli powder, salt, ginger and cornflour (cornstarch). Mix together thoroughly until the fish is well coated.

2 ▲ Heat the oil in a deep round-bottomed frying pan (skillet) or a medium karahi. Lower the heat slightly and add the fish pieces, 3 or 4 at a time. Fry for about 3 minutes, turning constantly.

3 Drain the fish pieces on kitchen paper (paper towels) and transfer to a serving dish. Keep warm and fry the remaining fish pieces.

4 ▲ Fry the (bell) peppers in the remaining oil for about 2 minutes. They should still be slightly crisp. Drain on kitchen paper.

5 Add the cooked peppers to the fish on the serving dish and garnish with the cherry tomatoes. Serve immediately with Raita and Paratha, if wished.

Balti Fish Fillets in Spicy Coconut Sauce

Use fresh fish fillets to make this dish if you can, as they have much more flavour than frozen ones. However, if you are using frozen fillets, ensure that they are completely thawed before using.

SERVES 4

INGREDIENTS
2 tbsp corn oil
1 tsp onion seeds
4 dried red chillies
3 garlic cloves, sliced
1 medium onion, sliced
2 medium tomatoes, sliced
2 tbsp desiccated (shredded) coconut
1 tsp salt
1 tsp ground coriander
*4 flatfish fillets, such as plaice, sole or
    flounder, each about 75 g/3 oz*
150 ml/¹/₄ pint/²/₃ cup water
1 tbsp lime juice
1 tbsp chopped fresh coriander (cilantro)

2 ▲ Add the tomatoes, coconut, salt and coriander and stir thoroughly.

3 ▲ Cut each fish fillet into 3 pieces. Drop the fish pieces into the mixture and turn them over gently until they are well coated.

4 Cook for 5–7 minutes, lowering the heat if necessary. Add the water, lime juice and fresh coriander (cilantro) and cook for a further 3–5 minutes until the water has mostly evaporated. Serve immediately with rice.

1 ▲ Heat the oil in a deep round-bottomed frying pan (skillet) or a karahi. Lower the heat slightly and add the onion seeds, dried red chillies, garlic slices and onion. Cook for 3–4 minutes, stirring once or twice.

Fish Fillets with a Chilli Sauce

LOW-FAT RECIPE

*For this recipe, the fish fillets are first
marinated with fresh coriander
(cilantro) and lemon juice, then cooked
under a hot grill (broiler) and served
with a chilli sauce. It is delicious
accompanied with Saffron and
Cardamom Flavoured Rice.*

SERVES 4

INGREDIENTS
*4 flatfish fillets, such as plaice, sole or
    flounder, about 115 g/4 oz each
2 tbsp lemon juice
1 tbsp finely chopped fresh coriander
    (cilantro)
1 tbsp vegetable oil
lime wedges
coriander (cilantro) sprig*

Sauce
*1 tsp ginger pulp
2 tbsp tomato purée (paste)
1 tsp sugar
1 tsp salt
1 tbsp chilli sauce
1 tbsp malt vinegar
300 ml/1/2 pint/ 1 1/4 cups water*

NUTRITIONAL VALUES (per portion)	
Total fat	5.28 g
Saturated fat	0.78 g
Cholesterol	47.25 mg
Energy (kcals/kj)	140/586

1 ▲ Rinse, pat dry and place the fish
fillets in a medium bowl. Add the
lemon juice, fresh coriander (cilantro)
and oil and rub into the fish. Leave to
marinate for at least 1 hour.

2 ▲ Mix together all the sauce
ingredients, pour into a small saucepan
and simmer over a low heat for about 6
minutes, stirring occasionally.

3 Preheat the grill (broiler) to medium.
Place the fillets under the grill for about
5–7 minutes.

4 ▲ When the fillets are cooked,
remove and arrange them on a warmed
serving dish.

5 The chilli sauce should now be fairly
thick – about the consistency of a thick
chicken soup.

6 ▲ Pour the sauce over the fillets,
garnish with the lime wedges and
coriander sprig and serve with rice.

VARIATION

*For a subtle change in flavour, substitute
the lemon juice in the marinade with an
equal quantity of lime juice.*

Balti Prawns (Shrimp) in Hot Sauce

This sizzling prawn (shrimp) dish is cooked in a fiery hot and spicy sauce. Not only does this sauce contain chilli powder, it is enhanced further by the addition of ground green chillies mixed with other spices. If the heat gets too much for anyone with a delicate palate, the addition of Raita will help to soften the piquant flavour.

SERVES 4

INGREDIENTS
2 medium onions, roughly chopped
2 tbsp tomato purée (paste)
1 tsp ground coriander
¼ tsp turmeric
1 tsp chilli powder
2 medium fresh green chillies
3 tbsp chopped fresh coriander (cilantro)
2 tbsp lemon juice
1 tsp salt
3 tbsp corn oil
16 cooked king prawns (jumbo shrimp)
1 fresh green chilli, chopped (optional)

1 ▲ Put the onions, tomato purée (paste), ground coriander, turmeric, chilli powder, 2 whole green chillies, 2 tbsp of the fresh coriander (cilantro), the lemon juice and salt into the bowl of a food processor. Process for about 1 minute. If the mixture seems too thick, add a little water to loosen it.

2 ▲ Heat the oil in a deep round-bottomed frying pan (skillet) or a karahi. Lower the heat slightly and add the spice mixture. Fry the mixture for 3–5 minutes or until the sauce has thickened slightly.

3 ▲ Add the prawns (shrimp) and stir-fry quickly over a medium heat.

4 As soon as the prawns are heated through, transfer them to a serving dish and garnish with the rest of the fresh coriander and the chopped green chilli, if using. Serve immediately.

COOK'S TIP

Cooked prawns (shrimp) have been used in all the seafood recipes. However, raw prawns – if you can find them – are especially delicious. Remove the black vein along the back of each prawn and extend the cooking time if necessary. The prawns will turn pink when they are cooked through.

Karahi Prawns (Shrimp) and Fenugreek

The black-eyed peas, prawns (shrimp) and paneer in this recipe mean that it is rich in protein. The combination of both ground and fresh fenugreek makes this a very fragrant and delicious dish. When preparing fresh fenugreek, use the leaves whole, but discard the stalks which would add a bitter flavour to the dish.

SERVES 4–6

INGREDIENTS
4 tbsp corn oil
2 medium onions, sliced
2 medium tomatoes, sliced
1½ tsp garlic pulp
1 tsp chilli powder
1 tsp ginger pulp
1 tsp ground cumin
1 tsp ground coriander
1 tsp salt
150 g/5 oz paneer, cubed
1 tsp ground fenugreek
1 bunch fresh fenugreek leaves
115 g/4 oz cooked prawns (shrimp)
2 fresh red chillies, sliced
2 tbsp chopped fresh coriander (cilantro)
50 g/2 oz/⅓ cup canned black-eye peas, drained
1 tbsp lemon juice

I ▲ Heat the oil in a deep round-bottomed frying pan (skillet) or a karahi. Lower the heat slightly and add the onions and tomatoes. Fry for about 3 minutes.

2 ▲ Add the garlic, chilli powder, ginger, ground cumin, ground coriander, salt, paneer and the ground and fresh fenugreek. Lower the heat and stir-fry for about 2 minutes.

3 ▲ Add the prawns (shrimp), red chillies, fresh coriander (cilantro) and the black-eyed peas and mix well. Cook for a further 3–5 minutes, stirring occasionally, or until the prawns are heated through.

4 Finally sprinkle on the lemon juice and serve.

Prawns (Shrimp) with Okra

This dish has a sweet taste with a strong chilli flavour. It should be cooked fast to prevent the okra from breaking up and releasing its distinctive, sticky interior.

SERVES 4–6

INGREDIENTS
4–6 tbsp oil
225 g/8 oz okra, washed, dried and left whole
4 cloves garlic, crushed
1 piece fresh ginger, 5 cm/2 in long, crushed
4–6 fresh green chillies, cut diagonally
½ tsp turmeric
4–6 curry leaves
1 tsp cumin seeds
450 g/1 lb fresh king prawns (jumbo shrimp), peeled and deveined
salt, to taste
2 tsp brown sugar
juice of 2 lemons

1 ▲ Heat the oil in a frying pan (skillet) and fry the okra over a fairly high heat until they are slightly crisp and browned on all sides. Remove from the oil and put to one side on a piece of kitchen paper (paper towel).

2 In the same oil, gently fry the garlic, ginger, chillies, turmeric, curry leaves and cumin seeds for 2–3 minutes. Add the prawns (shrimp) and mix well. Cook until the prawns are tender.

3 ▲ Add the salt, sugar, lemon juice and fried okra. Increase the heat and quickly fry for a further 5 minutes, stirring gently to prevent the okra from breaking. Adjust the seasoning, if necessary. Serve hot.

Fried Whole Fish

In southern India, fish is prepared daily in some form or other but most often it is just fried and served with a lentil curry and a nice hot pickle.

SERVES 4–6

INGREDIENTS
1 small onion, coarsely chopped
4 cloves garlic
1 piece fresh ginger, 5 cm/2 in long, chopped
1 tsp turmeric
2 tsp chilli powder
salt, to taste
4 red mullet
vegetable oil, for shallow-frying
1 tsp cumin seeds
3 fresh green chillies, finely sliced
lime slices, to serve

1 ▲ Using a food processor, grind the first 6 ingredients to a smooth paste. Make gashes on both sides of the fish and rub them with the paste. Leave to rest for 1 hour in a cool place. Lightly pat the fish dry with kitchen paper (paper towel) without removing the paste. Excess fluid will be released as the salt dissolves.

2 ▲ Heat the oil in a large frying pan (skillet) and fry the cumin seeds and chillies for about 1 minute. Fry the fish in batches. When the first side is sealed, turn the fish over very gently to ensure they do not break. Fry until they are golden brown on both sides, drain well and serve hot with lime slices.

Prawns (Shrimp) with Okra (top) and Fried Whole Fish

Paneer Balti with Prawns (Shrimp)

Although paneer is not widely eaten in Pakistan, it makes an excellent substitute for red meat. Here it is combined with king prawns (jumbo shrimp) to make one of my favourite dishes.

SERVES 4

INGREDIENTS
12 cooked king prawns (jumbo shrimp)
175 g/6 oz paneer
2 tbsp tomato purée (paste)
4 tbsp Greek-style yogurt
1½ tsp garam masala
1 tsp chilli powder
1 tsp garlic pulp
1 tsp salt
2 tsp mango powder
1 tsp ground coriander
115 g/4 oz/8 tbsp butter
1 tbsp corn oil
3 fresh green chillies, chopped
3 tbsp chopped fresh coriander (cilantro)
150 ml/¼ pint/⅔ cup single (light) cream

1 ▲ Peel the king prawns (jumbo shrimp) and cube the paneer.

2 Blend the tomato purée (paste), yogurt, garam masala, chilli powder, garlic, salt, mango powder and ground coriander in a mixing bowl and set to one side.

3 ▲ Melt the butter with the oil in a deep round-bottomed frying pan (skillet) or a medium karahi. Lower the heat slightly and quickly fry the paneer and prawns for about 2 minutes. Remove with a slotted spoon and drain on kitchen paper (paper towels).

4 ▲ Pour the spice mixture into the fat left in the pan and stir-fry for about 1 minute.

5 ▲ Add the paneer and prawns, and cook for 7–10 minutes, stirring occasionally, until the prawns are heated through.

6 ▲ Add the fresh chillies and most of the coriander (cilantro), and pour in the cream. Heat through for about 2 minutes, garnish with the remaining coriander and serve.

HOME-MADE PANEER

To make paneer at home, bring 1 litre/1¾ pints/4 cups milk to the boil over a low heat. Add 2 tbsp lemon juice, stirring continuously and gently until the milk thickens and begins to curdle. Strain the curdled milk through a sieve (strainer) lined with muslin (cheesecloth). Set aside under a heavy weight for about 1½–2 hours to press to a flat shape about 1 cm/½ in thick.

Make the paneer a day before you plan to use it in a recipe; it will then be firmer and easier to handle. Cut and use as required; it will keep for about one week in the refrigerator.

Grilled (Broiled) Fish Fillets

LOW-FAT RECIPE

The nice thing about fish is that it can be grilled (broiled) beautifully without sacrificing any flavour. For this recipe I have used a minimum amount of oil to baste the fish.

SERVES 4

INGREDIENTS

*4 medium flatfish fillets, such as plaice, sole or flounder, about 115 g/
    4 oz each
1 tsp garlic pulp
1 tsp garam masala
1 tsp chilli powder
¼ tsp turmeric
½ tsp salt
1 tbsp finely chopped fresh coriander
    (cilantro)
1 tbsp vegetable oil
2 tbsp lemon juice*

NUTRITIONAL VALUES (per portion)	
Total fat	5.63 g
Saturated fat	0.84 g
Cholesterol	47.25 mg
Energy (kcals/kj)	143/599

1 ▲ Line a flameproof dish or grill (broiler) tray with foil. Rinse and pat dry the fish fillets and put them on the foil-lined dish or tray.

2 ▲ In a small bowl, mix together the garlic, garam masala, chilli powder, turmeric, salt, fresh coriander (cilantro), oil and lemon juice.

3 ▲ Using a pastry brush, baste the fish fillets evenly all over with the spice and lemon juice mixture.

4 Preheat the grill to very hot, then lower the heat to medium. Grill (broil) the fillets for about 10 minutes, basting occasionally, until they are cooked right through.

5 Serve immediately with an attractive garnish, such as grated carrot, tomato quarters and lime slices, if wished.

Glazed Garlic Prawns (Shrimp)

A fairly simple and quick dish to prepare, it is best to peel the prawns (shrimp) as this helps them to absorb maximum flavour. Serve as a main course with accompaniments, or with a salad as an appetizer.

SERVES 4

INGREDIENTS
1 tbsp vegetable oil
3 garlic cloves, roughly chopped
3 tomatoes, chopped
½ tsp salt
1 tsp crushed dried red chillies
1 tsp lemon juice
1 tbsp mango chutney
1 fresh green chilli, chopped
15–20 cooked king prawns (jumbo shrimp), peeled
fresh coriander (cilantro) sprigs
2 spring onions (scallions), chopped (optional)

NUTRITIONAL VALUES (per portion)	
Total fat	3.83 g
Saturated fat	0.54 g
Cholesterol	30.37 mg
Energy (kcals/kj)	90/380

1 ▲ In a medium saucepan, heat the oil and add the chopped garlic.

2 ▲ Lower the heat and add the chopped tomatoes along with the salt, crushed chillies, lemon juice, mango chutney and chopped fresh chilli.

3 ▲ Finally add the prawns (shrimp), turn up the heat and stir-fry these quickly, until heated through.

4 Transfer to a serving dish. Serve garnished with fresh coriander (cilantro) sprigs and chopped spring onions (scallions), if wished.

Balti Prawns (Shrimp) and Vegetables in Thick Sauce

Here, tender prawns (shrimp), crunchy vegetables and a thick curry sauce combine to produce a dish rich in flavour and texture. Fruity Pullao is a perfect accompaniment, although plain rice is a good alternative.

SERVES 4

INGREDIENTS

3 tbsp corn oil
1 tsp mixed fenugreek, mustard and onion seeds
2 curry leaves
1/2 medium cauliflower, cut into small florets (flowerets)
8 baby carrots, halved lengthways
6 new potatoes, thickly sliced
50 g/2 oz/1/2 cup frozen peas
2 medium onions, sliced
2 tbsp tomato purée (paste)
1 1/2 tsp chilli powder
1 tsp ground coriander
1 tsp ginger pulp
1 tsp garlic pulp
1 tsp salt
2 tbsp lemon juice
450 g/1 lb cooked prawns (shrimp)
2 tbsp chopped fresh coriander (cilantro)
1 fresh red chilli, seeded and sliced
120 ml/4 fl oz/1/2 cup single (light) cream

2 ▲ Turn up the heat and add the cauliflower, carrots, potatoes and peas. Stir-fry quickly until browned, then remove from the pan with a slotted spoon and drain on kitchen paper (paper towels).

3 Add the onions to the oil left in the karahi and fry over a medium heat until golden brown.

4 ▲ While the onions are cooking, mix together the tomato purée (paste), chilli powder, ground coriander, ginger, garlic, salt and lemon juice and pour the paste onto the onions.

5 Add the prawns (shrimp) and stir-fry over a low heat for about 5 minutes or until they are heated through.

6 ▲ Add the fried vegetables to the pan and mix together well.

7 ▲ Add the fresh coriander (cilantro) and red chilli and pour over the cream. Bring to the boil and serve immediately.

VARIATION

Monkfish is an excellent alternative to the prawns (shrimp) used in this recipe, as it is a firm-fleshed fish that will not break up when fried. Cut the monkfish into chunks, add to the onion and spice mixture at step 5 and stir-fry over a low heat for 5–7 minutes or until the fish is cooked through.

1 ▲ Heat the oil in a deep round-bottomed frying pan (skillet) or a large karahi. Lower the heat slightly and add the fenugreek, mustard and onion seeds and the curry leaves.

Stuffed Fish

Every community in India prepares stuffed fish but the Parsi version must rank top of the list. The most popular fish in India is the pomfret. These are available from Indian and Chinese grocers or large supermarkets.

SERVES 4

INGREDIENTS
2 large pomfrets, or Dover or lemon sole
2 tsp salt
juice of 1 lemon

Masala
8 tbsp desiccated (shredded) coconut
115 g/4 oz/4 cups fresh coriander (cilantro), including the tender stalks
8 fresh green chillies (or to taste)
1 tsp cumin seeds
6 cloves garlic
2 tsp sugar
2 tsp lemon juice

I ▲ Scale the fish and cut off the fins. Gut the fish and remove the heads, if desired. Using a sharp knife, make 2 diagonal gashes on each side, then pat dry with kitchen paper (paper towel).

2 ▲ Rub the fish inside and out with salt and lemon juice and allow to stand in a cool place for about 1 hour. Pat dry thoroughly.

3 ▲ For the masala, grind all the ingredients together using a pestle and mortar or food processor. Stuff the fish with the masala mixture and rub any remaining into the gashes and all over the fish on both sides.

4 ▲ Place each fish on a separate piece of greased foil. Tightly wrap the foil over each fish. Place in a steamer and steam for 20 minutes, or bake for 30 minutes at 200°C/400°F/Gas 6 or until cooked. Remove the fish from the foil and serve hot.

COOK'S TIP

In India, this fish dish is always steamed wrapped in banana leaves. Banana leaves are generally available from Indian or Chinese grocers but vine leaves from Greek food shops could be used instead.

Parsi Prawn (Shrimp) Curry

This dish comes from the west coast of India, where fresh seafood is eaten in abundance. Fresh king prawns (jumbo shrimp) or 'tiger' prawns are ideal.

SERVES 4–6

INGREDIENTS
4 tbsp vegetable oil
1 medium onion, finely sliced
6 cloves garlic, finely crushed
1 tsp chilli powder
1 1/2 tsp turmeric
2 medium onions, finely chopped
4 tbsp tamarind juice
1 tsp mint sauce
1 tbsp demerara sugar
salt, to taste
450 g/1 lb fresh king prawns (jumbo shrimp), peeled and deveined
75 g/3 oz/3 cups fresh coriander (cilantro), chopped

1 ▲ Heat the oil in a frying pan (skillet) and fry the sliced onion until golden brown. In a bowl, mix the garlic, chilli powder and turmeric with a little water to form a paste. Add to the browned onion and simmer for 3 minutes.

2 ▲ Add the chopped onions to the pan and fry until they become translucent, stirring frequently. Stir in the tamarind juice, mint sauce, sugar and salt and gently simmer for a further 3 minutes.

3 ▲ Pat the prawns (shrimp) dry with kitchen paper (paper towel). Add to the spice mixture with a small amount of water and stir-fry until the prawns turn a bright orange/pink colour.

4 ▲ When the prawns are cooked, add the fresh coriander (cilantro) and stir-fry over a high heat for a few minutes to thicken the sauce. Serve hot.

Prawn (Shrimp) and Spinach Pancakes (Crêpes)

LOW-FAT RECIPE

Serve these delicious filled pancakes (crêpes) hot with the Spicy Baby Vegetable Salad. Try to use red onions for this recipe, although they are not essential.

MAKES 4–6 PANCAKES (CRÊPES)

INGREDIENTS
Pancakes (Crêpes)
175 g/6 oz/1½ cups plain (all-purpose) flour
½ tsp salt
3 eggs
1½ cups semi-skimmed (2%) milk
15 g/½ oz/1 tbsp low-fat margarine

Filling
2 tbsp vegetable oil
2 medium red onions, sliced
½ tsp garlic pulp
2.5 cm/1 in piece ginger, shredded
1 tsp chilli powder
1 tsp garam masala
1 tsp salt
2 tomatoes, sliced
225 g/8 oz frozen leaf spinach, thawed and drained
115 g/4 oz cooked prawns (shrimp)
2 tbsp chopped fresh coriander (cilantro)

Garnish
1 tomato, quartered
fresh coriander (cilantro) sprigs
lemon wedges

NUTRITIONAL VALUES (per portion)

Total fat	14.04 g
Saturated fat	3.19 g
Cholesterol	173.33 mg
Energy (kcals/kj)	373/1568

1 ▲ To make the pancakes (crêpes), sift the flour and salt together. Beat the eggs and add to the flour, beating continuously. Gradually stir in the milk. Leave to stand for 1 hour.

2 Heat the oil in a deep frying pan (skillet) and fry the sliced onions over a medium heat until golden.

3 ▲ Gradually add the garlic, ginger, chilli powder, garam masala and salt, followed by the tomatoes and spinach, stir-frying constantly.

4 ▲ Add the prawns (shrimp) and fresh coriander (cilantro). Cook for a further 5–7 minutes or until any excess water has been absorbed. Keep warm.

5 ▲ Heat about ½ tsp of the low-fat margarine in a 25 cm/10 in non-stick frying pan (skillet) or pancake pan. Pour in about one-quarter of the pancake batter, tilting the pan so the batter spreads well, coats the bottom of the pan and is evenly distributed.

6 ▲ When fine bubbles begin to appear on top, flip it over using a spatula and cook for a further minute or so. Transfer to a plate and keep warm. Cook the remaining pancakes in the same way.

7 Fill the pancakes with the spinach and prawns and garnish with the tomato and fresh coriander sprigs. Serve warm with lemon wedges.

Seafood Balti with Vegetables

In this dish, the spicy seafood is cooked separately and combined with the vegetables at the last minute to give a truly delicious combination of flavours.

SERVES 4

INGREDIENTS
Seafood
225 g/¹/₂ lb cod, or any other firm, white fish
225 g/¹/₂ lb cooked prawns (shrimp)
6 crab sticks, halved lengthways
1 tbsp lemon juice
1 tsp ground coriander
1 tsp chilli powder
1 tsp salt
1 tsp ground cumin
4 tbsp cornflour (cornstarch)
150 ml/¹/₄ pint/²/₃ cup corn oil

Vegetables
150 ml/¹/₄ pint/²/₃ cup corn oil
2 medium onions, chopped
1 tsp onion seeds
¹/₂ medium cauliflower, cut into florets (flowerets)
115 g/4 oz French (green) beans, cut into 2.5 cm/1 in lengths
175 g/6 oz/1 cup sweetcorn (corn kernels)
1 tsp shredded ginger
1 tsp chilli powder
1 tsp salt
4 fresh green chillies, sliced
2 tbsp chopped fresh coriander (cilantro)
lime slices

I Skin the fish and cut into small cubes. Put into a medium mixing bowl with the prawns (shrimps) and crab sticks, and put to one side.

2 ▲ In a separate bowl, mix together the lemon juice, ground coriander, chilli powder, salt and ground cumin. Pour this over the seafood and mix together thoroughly using your hands.

3 Sprinkle on the cornflour (cornstarch) and mix again until the seafood is well coated. Set to one side in the refrigerator for about 1 hour to allow the flavours to develop.

4 ▲ To make the vegetable mixture, heat the oil in a deep round-bottomed frying pan (skillet) or a karahi. Throw in the onions and the onion seeds, and stir-fry until lightly browned.

5 Add the cauliflower, French (green) beans, sweetcorn (corn kernels), ginger, chilli powder, salt, green chillies and fresh coriander (cilantro). Stir-fry for about 7–10 minutes over a medium heat, making sure that the cauliflower florets (flowerets) retain their shape.

6 ▲ Spoon the fried vegetables around the edge of a shallow dish, leaving a space in the middle for the seafood, and keep warm.

7 ▲ Wash and dry the pan, then heat the oil to fry the seafood pieces. Fry the seafood pieces in 2–3 batches, until they turn a golden brown. Remove with a slotted spoon and drain on kitchen paper (paper towels).

8 Arrange the seafood in the middle of the dish of vegetables and keep warm while you fry the remaining seafood. Garnish with lime slices and serve. Plain boiled rice and Raita make ideal accompaniments.

Prawns (Shrimp) with Vegetables

LOW-FAT RECIPE

This is a light and nutritious dish, excellent served either on a bed of lettuce leaves, with plain boiled rice or Wholemeal (Whole-Wheat) Chapatis.

SERVES 4

INGREDIENTS
2 tbsp chopped fresh coriander (cilantro)
1 tsp salt
2 fresh green chillies, seeded if wished
3 tbsp lemon juice
2 tbsp vegetable oil
20 cooked king prawns (jumbo shrimp), peeled
1 medium courgette (zucchini), thickly sliced
1 medium onion, cut into 8 chunks
8 cherry tomatoes
8 baby corn cobs
mixed salad leaves

NUTRITIONAL VALUES (per portion)	
Total fat	6.47 g
Saturated fat	0.85 g
Cholesterol	29.16 mg
Energy (kcals/kj)	109/458

1 ▲ Place the chopped coriander (cilantro), salt, green chillies, lemon juice and oil in a food processor and grind these together for a few seconds.

2 ▲ Remove the contents from the processor and transfer to a medium mixing bowl.

3 ▲ Add the peeled prawns (shrimp) to this mixture and stir to make sure that all the prawns are well coated. Set aside to marinate for about 30 minutes.

4 Preheat the grill (broiler) to very hot, then turn the heat down to medium.

5 ▲ Arrange the vegetables and prawns alternately on 4 skewers. When all the skewers are ready place them under the preheated grill for 5–7 minutes until cooked and browned.

6 Serve immediately on a bed of mixed salad leaves.

COOK'S TIP

King prawns (jumbo shrimp) are a luxury, but worth choosing for a special dinner. For a more economical variation, substitute the king prawns with 450 g/1 lb ordinary prawns.

Bombay Duck Pickle

*B*omil is an unusual fish found off the west coast of India during the monsoon season. It is salted and dried in the sun and is characterized by a strong smell and distinctive piquancy. How this fish acquired the name Bombay duck in the Western world still remains a mystery!

SERVES 4–6

INGREDIENTS
6–8 pieces bomil (Bombay duck), soaked
    in water for 5 minutes
4 tbsp vegetable oil
2 fresh red chillies, chopped
1 tbsp sugar
450 g/1 lb cherry tomatoes, halved
115 g/4 oz deep-fried onions

1 ▲ Pat the soaked fish dry with kitchen paper (paper towel). Heat the oil in a frying pan (skillet) and fry the Bombay duck pieces for about 30–45 seconds on both sides until crisp. Be careful not to burn them or they will taste bitter. Drain well on kitchen paper. When cool, break the fish into small pieces.

2 ▲ In the same oil, cook the remaining ingredients until the tomatoes become pulpy and the onions are blended into a sauce. Fold in the Bombay duck pieces and serve hot or cold.

Fish Cakes

*T*hese tasty fish cakes can be made slightly larger and served as fish burgers, or made into small balls to serve as cocktail snacks.

MAKES 20

INGREDIENTS
450 g/1 lb firm, white fish, skinned
2 medium potatoes, peeled, boiled and
    mashed
4 spring onions (scallions), finely chopped
4 fresh green chillies, finely chopped
1 piece fresh ginger, 5 cm/2 in long, finely
    crushed
few fresh coriander (cilantro) and mint
    leaves, chopped
salt and freshly ground black pepper, to
    taste
2 eggs
breadcrumbs, for coating
vegetable oil, for shallow-frying
chilli sauce or sweet chutney, to serve
lemon wedges, to serve

1 ▲ Place the fish in a lightly greased steamer and steam until cooked. Remove the pan from the heat.

2 ▲ Place the potatoes, spring onions (scallions), spices, fresh coriander and mint, seasonings and 1 egg in a large bowl. When the fish is cool, crumble it coarsely into the bowl and mix well.

3 ▲ Shape the mixture into cakes. Beat the remaining egg and dip the cakes in it, then coat with the breadcrumbs. Heat the oil and fry the cakes until brown on all sides.

Bombay Duck Pickle (top) and Fish Cakes

Vegetable Dishes

The range of vegetables available today lends inspiration for side dishes, and both subtle and hot spicing will enhance their fresh flavour. Choose from everyday accompaniments like Curried Cauliflower or Bombay Potatoes, one of the delicious main meal vegetable curries, or try a more unusual side dish such as Okra in Yogurt or Karahi Shredded Cabbage.

Okra in Yogurt

This tangy vegetable dish can be served as an accompaniment, but also makes an excellent vegetarian meal served with Tarka Dhal and Wholemeal (Whole-Wheat) Chapatis.

SERVES 4

INGREDIENTS
450 g/1 lb okra
2 tbsp corn oil
½ tsp onion seeds
3 medium fresh green chillies, chopped
1 medium onion, sliced
¼ tsp turmeric
2 tsp desiccated (shredded) coconut
½ tsp salt
1 tbsp natural (plain) low-fat yogurt
2 medium tomatoes, sliced
1 tbsp chopped fresh coriander (cilantro)

NUTRITIONAL VALUES (per portion)

Total fat	8.44 g
Saturated fat	2.09 g
Cholesterol	0.15 mg
Energy (kcals/kj)	119/501

1 ▲ Wash, top and tail the okra, cut into 1 cm/½ in pieces and set aside.

2 ▲ Heat the oil in a medium frying pan (skillet), add the onion seeds, green chillies and onion and fry for about 5 minutes until the onion has turned golden brown.

3 ▲ Lower the heat and add the turmeric, desiccated (shredded) coconut and salt and fry for about 1 minute.

4 ▲ Next add the okra, turn the heat to medium-high and quickly stir-fry for a few minutes until lightly golden.

5 ▲ Add the yogurt, tomatoes and finally the fresh coriander (cilantro). Cook for a further 2 minutes.

6 Transfer onto a serving dish and serve immediately.

Bombay Potatoes

This authentic dish belongs to the Gujerati, a totally vegetarian sect and the largest population in Bombay.

SERVES 4–6

INGREDIENTS
450 g/1 lb new potatoes
salt, to taste
1 tsp turmeric
4 tbsp vegetable oil
2 dried red chillies
6–8 curry leaves
2 onions, finely chopped
2 fresh green chillies, finely chopped
*50 g/2 oz/2 cups fresh coriander
   (cilantro), coarsely chopped*
¼ tsp asafoetida
*½ tsp each, cumin, mustard, onion, fennel
   and nigella seeds*
lemon juice, to taste

1 Scrub the potatoes under cold running water and cut them into small pieces. Boil the potatoes in water with a little salt and ½ tsp of the turmeric for 10–15 minutes, or until tender. Drain the potatoes well then mash. Put aside.

2 ▲ Heat the oil in a frying pan (skillet) and fry the dried chillies and curry leaves until the chillies are nearly burnt. Add the onions, green chillies, fresh coriander (cilantro), remaining turmeric and spice seeds and cook until the onions are soft.

3 ▲ Fold in the potatoes and add a few drops of water. Cook over a low heat for about 10 minutes, stirring well to ensure the spices are evenly mixed. Add lemon juice to taste, and serve.

Curried Cauliflower

In this dish the creamy coconut sauce complements the flavour of the spiced cauliflower.

SERVES 4–6

INGREDIENTS
1 tbsp gram flour (besan)
120 ml/4 fl oz/½ cup water
1 tsp chilli powder
1 tbsp ground coriander
1 tsp ground cumin
1 tsp mustard powder
1 tsp turmeric
salt, to taste
4 tbsp vegetable oil
6–8 curry leaves
1 tsp cumin seeds
*1 cauliflower, broken into florets
   (flowerets)*
175 ml/6 fl oz/¾ cup thick coconut milk

juice of 2 lemons
lime wedges, to serve

1 ▲ Mix the gram flour with a little of the water to make a smooth paste. Add the chilli, coriander, cumin, mustard, turmeric and salt. Add the remaining water and keep mixing to blend all the ingredients well.

2 Heat the oil in a frying pan (skillet), add the curry leaves and cumin seeds. Add the spice paste and simmer for about 5 minutes. If the sauce has become too thick, add a little hot water.

3 ▲ Add the cauliflower and coconut milk. Bring to the boil, reduce the heat, cover and cook until the cauliflower is tender but crunchy. Cook longer if you prefer. Add the lemon juice, mix well and serve hot with the lime wedges.

Bombay Potatoes (top) and Curried Cauliflower

Courgettes (Zucchini) with Mushrooms in a Creamy Sauce

LOW-FAT RECIPE

When cream and mushrooms are cooked together they complement each other beautifully. Though this dish sounds very rich, by using single (light) cream and very little oil you can keep the fat content to a minimum.

SERVES 4

INGREDIENTS
2 tbsp vegetable oil
1 medium onion, roughly chopped
1 tsp ground coriander
1 tsp ground cumin
1 tsp salt
½ tsp chilli powder
225 g/8 oz/3 cups mushrooms, sliced
2 medium courgettes (zucchini), sliced
3 tbsp single (light) cream
1 tbsp chopped fresh coriander (cilantro)

1 ▲ Heat the oil and fry the chopped onions until golden brown. Lower the heat to medium, add the ground coriander, cumin, salt and chilli powder and stir together well.

NUTRITIONAL VALUES (per portion)	
Total fat	7.73 g
Saturated fat	1.80 g
Cholesterol	4.50 mg
Energy (kcals/kj)	95/400

2 ▲ Once the onions and the spices are well blended, add the mushrooms and courgettes (zucchini) and stir-fry gently for about 5 minutes until soft. If the mixture is too dry just add a little water to loosen.

3 ▲ Finally pour in the cream and mix it well into the vegetables.

4 Garnish with fresh chopped coriander (cilantro), if wished, and serve immediately.

Potatoes with Red Chillies

LOW-FAT RECIPE

The quantity of red chillies used here may be too fiery for some palates. For a milder version, either seed the chillies, use fewer or substitute them with 1 roughly chopped red (bell) pepper.

SERVES 4

INGREDIENTS
12–14 baby new potatoes, peeled and
   halved
2 tbsp vegetable oil
½ tsp crushed dried red chillies
½ tsp white cumin seeds
½ tsp fennel seeds
½ tsp crushed coriander seeds
1 tbsp salt
1 medium onion, sliced
1–4 fresh red chillies, chopped
1 tbsp chopped fresh coriander (cilantro)

NUTRITIONAL VALUES (per portion)	
Total fat	6.31 g
Saturated fat	0.75 g
Cholesterol	0.00 mg
Energy (kcals/kj)	151/634

1 ▲ Boil the baby potatoes in salted water until soft but still firm. Remove from the heat and drain off the water.

2 ▲ In a deep frying pan (skillet), heat the oil, then turn down the heat to medium. Then add the crushed chillies, cumin, fennel and coriander seeds and salt and fry for 30–40 seconds.

3 ▼ Add the sliced onion and fry until golden brown. Then add the potatoes, red chillies and fresh coriander (cilantro).

4 Cover and cook for 5–7 minutes over a very low heat. Serve hot.

Balti Baby Vegetables

There is a wide and wonderful selection of baby vegetables available in supermarkets these days, and this simple recipe does full justice to their delicate flavour and attractive appearance. Serve as part of a main meal or even as a light appetizer.

SERVES 4–6

INGREDIENTS
10 new potatoes, halved
12–14 baby carrots
12–14 baby courgettes (zucchini)
2 tbsp corn oil
15 baby onions
2 tbsp chilli sauce
1 tsp garlic pulp
1 tsp ginger pulp
1 tsp salt
400 g/14 oz/2 cups canned chick-peas (garbanzos), drained
10 cherry tomatoes
1 tsp crushed dried red chillies
2 tbsp sesame seeds

1 ▲ Bring a medium pan of salted water to the boil and add the potatoes and carrots. After about 12–15 minutes, add the courgettes (zucchini) and boil for a further 5 minutes or until all the vegetables are just tender.

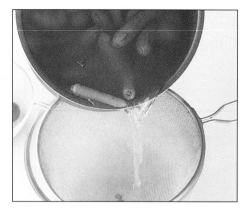

2 ▲ Drain the vegetables well and set to one side.

3 ▲ Heat the oil in a deep round-bottomed frying pan (skillet) or a karahi and add the baby onions. Fry until the onions turn golden brown. Lower the heat and add the chilli sauce, garlic, ginger and salt, taking care not to burn the mixture.

4 ▲ Add the chick-peas (garbanzos) and stir-fry over a medium heat until the moisture has been absorbed.

5 ▲ Add the cooked vegetables and cherry tomatoes and stir over the heat with a slotted spoon for about 2 minutes.

6 Add the crushed red chillies and sesame seeds as a garnish and serve.

VARIATION

By varying the vegetables chosen and experimenting with different combinations, this recipe can form the basis for a wide variety of vegetable accompaniments. Try baby corn cobs, French (green) beans, mange-tout (snow peas), okra and cauliflower florets (flowerets), too.

Stuffed Okra

A delicious accompaniment to any dish, this can also be served on a bed of strained yogurt which gives an excellent contrast in flavour.

SERVES 4–6

INGREDIENTS
225 g/8 oz large okra
1 tbsp mango powder
½ tsp ground ginger
½ tsp ground cumin
½ tsp chilli powder (optional)
½ tsp turmeric
salt, to taste
a few drops of vegetable oil
2 tbsp cornflour (cornstarch), placed in a
    plastic bag
vegetable oil, for frying

I ▲ Wash the okra and dry on kitchen paper (paper towel). Carefully trim off the tops without making a hole. Using a sharp knife, make a slit lengthways in the centre of each okra but do not cut all the way through.

2 ▲ In a bowl, mix the mango powder, ginger, cumin, chilli if using, turmeric and salt with a few drops of oil. Leave the mixture to rest for 1–2 hours.

3 ▲ Using your fingers, part the slit of each okra carefully and fill each with as much of the spice filling as possible.

4 Put all the okra into the plastic bag with the cornflour (cornstarch) and shake the bag carefully to cover the okra evenly.

5 ▲ Fill the frying pan (skillet) with enough oil to sit 2.5 cm/1 in deep, heat it and fry the okra in small batches for about 5–8 minutes or until they are brown and slightly crisp. Serve hot.

Mixed Vegetable Curry

This is a very delicately spiced vegetable dish that makes an appetizing snack when served with plain yogurt. It is also a good accompaniment to a main meal of heavily spiced curries.

SERVES 4–6

INGREDIENTS
350 g/12 oz mixed vegetables, eg beans, peas, potatoes, cauliflower, carrots, cabbage, mange-touts (snow peas) and button mushrooms
2 tbsp vegetable oil
1 tsp cumin seeds, freshly roasted
½ tsp mustard seeds
½ tsp onion seeds
1 tsp turmeric
2 cloves garlic, crushed
6–8 curry leaves
1 dried red chilli
salt, to taste
1 tsp sugar
150 ml/¼ pint/⅔ cup natural (plain) yogurt mixed with 1 tsp cornflour (cornstarch)

1 ▲ Prepare all the vegetables you have chosen: string the beans; thaw the peas, if frozen; cube the potatoes; cut the cauliflower into florets (flowerets); dice the carrots; shred the cabbage; top and tail the mange-touts (snow peas); wash the mushrooms and leave whole.

2 ▲ Heat a large pan with enough water to cook all the vegetables and bring to the boil. First add the potatoes and carrots and cook until nearly tender then add all the other vegetables and cook until still firm. All the vegetables should be crunchy except the potatoes. Drain well.

3 ▲ Heat the oil in a frying pan (skillet) and fry the cumin, mustard and onion seeds, the turmeric, garlic, curry leaves and dried chilli gently until the garlic is golden brown and the chilli nearly burnt. Reduce the heat.

4 ▲ Fold in the drained vegetables, add the sugar and salt and gradually add the yogurt mixed with the cornflour (cornstarch). Heat to serving temperature and serve immediately.

Potatoes in a Yogurt Sauce

It is nice to use tiny new potatoes with the skins on for this recipe. The yogurt adds a tangy flavour to this fairly spicy dish, which is delicious served with Wholemeal (Whole-Wheat) Chapatis.

SERVES 4

INGREDIENTS
12 new potatoes, halved
275 g/10 oz/1¼ cups natural (plain)
    low-fat yogurt
300 ml/½ pint/1¼ cups water
¼ tsp turmeric
1 tsp chilli powder
1 tsp ground coriander
½ tsp ground cumin
1 tsp salt
1 tsp soft brown sugar
2 tbsp vegetable oil
1 tsp white cumin seeds
1 tbsp chopped fresh coriander (cilantro)
2 fresh green chillies, sliced
1 fresh coriander sprig (optional)

NUTRITIONAL VALUES (per portion)	
Total fat	6.84 g
Saturated fat	1.11 g
Cholesterol	2.80 mg
Energy (kcals/kj)	184/774

1 ▲ Boil the potatoes in salted water with their skins on until they are just tender, then drain and set aside.

2 ▲ Mix together the yogurt, water, turmeric, chilli powder, ground coriander, ground cumin, salt and sugar in a bowl. Set aside.

3 ▲ Heat the oil in a medium saucepan and add the white cumin seeds.

4 ▲ Reduce the heat, stir in the yogurt mixture and cook for about 3 minutes over a medium heat.

5 ▲ Add the fresh coriander (cilantro), green chillies and cooked potatoes. Blend everything together and cook for a further 5–7 minutes, stirring occasionally.

6 Transfer to a serving dish and garnish with the coriander sprig, if wished.

COOK'S TIP

If new potatoes are unavailable, use 450 g/2 lb ordinary potatoes instead. Peel them and cut into large chunks, then cook as described above.

Spinach and Potatoes

India is blessed with over 18 varieties of spinach. If you have access to an Indian or Chinese grocer, look out for some of the more unusual varieties.

SERVES 4–6

INGREDIENTS

4 tbsp vegetable oil
225 g/8 oz potatoes
1 piece fresh ginger, 2.5 cm/1 in long,
   crushed
4 cloves garlic, crushed
1 onion, coarsely chopped
2 fresh green chillies, chopped
2 dried red chillies, coarsely broken
1 tsp cumin seeds
salt, to taste
225 g/8 oz fresh spinach, trimmed, washed
   and chopped or 225 g/8 oz frozen
   spinach, thawed and drained
2 firm tomatoes, coarsely chopped,
   to garnish

1 ▲ Wash the potatoes and cut into quarters. If using small new potatoes, leave them whole. Heat the oil in a frying pan (skillet) and fry the potatoes until brown on all sides. Remove and put aside.

2 ▲ Remove the excess oil leaving about 1 tbsp in the pan. Fry the ginger, garlic, onion, green chillies, dried chillies and cumin seeds until the onion is golden brown.

3 ▲ Add the potatoes and salt and stir well. Cover the pan and cook over a medium heat, stirring occasionally, until the potatoes are tender when pierced with a sharp knife.

4 ▲ Add the spinach and stir well. Cook with the pan uncovered until the spinach is tender and all the excess fluids have evaporated. Garnish with the chopped tomatoes and serve hot.

Mushrooms, Peas and Paneer

Paneer is a traditional cheese made from rich milk and is most popular with northern Indians. Rajasthani farmers eat this dish for lunch with thick parathas as they work in the fields.

SERVES 4–6

INGREDIENTS
6 tbsp ghee or vegetable oil
225 g/8 oz paneer, cubed
1 onion, finely chopped
few mint leaves, chopped
50 g/2 oz/2 cups fresh coriander (cilantro), chopped
3 fresh green chillies, chopped
3 cloves garlic
1 piece fresh ginger, 2.5 cm/1 in long, sliced
1 tsp turmeric
1 tsp chilli powder (optional)
1 tsp garam masala
salt, to taste
225 g/8 oz/3 cups tiny button mushrooms, washed and left whole
225 g/8 oz/1½ cups frozen peas, thawed and drained
175 ml/6 fl oz/¾ cup natural (plain) yogurt, mixed with 1 tsp cornflour (cornstarch)
mint sprig, to garnish

2 ▲ Grind the onion, mint, coriander (cilantro), chillies, garlic and ginger in a pestle and mortar or food processor to a fairly smooth paste. Remove and mix in the turmeric, chilli powder if using, garam masala and salt.

3 ▲ Remove excess ghee or oil from the pan leaving about 1 tbsp. Heat and fry the paste until the raw onion smell disappears and the oil separates.

4 ▲ Add the mushrooms, peas and paneer. Mix well. Cool the mixture and gradually fold in the yogurt. Simmer for about 10 minutes. Garnish with a sprig of mint and serve hot.

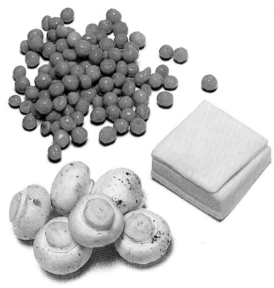

1 ▲ Heat the ghee or oil in a frying pan (skillet) and fry the paneer cubes until they are golden brown on all sides. Remove and drain on kitchen paper (paper towel).

Masala Mashed Potatoes

These potatoes are very versatile and will perk up any meal.

SERVES 4

INGREDIENTS
3 medium potatoes
1 tbsp chopped fresh mint and coriander
  (cilantro), mixed
1 tsp mango powder
1 tsp salt
1 tsp crushed black peppercorns
1 fresh red chilli, chopped
1 fresh green chilli, chopped
50 g/2 oz/4 tbsp low-fat margarine

NUTRITIONAL VALUES (per portion)	
Total fat	5.80 g
Saturated fat	1.25 g
Cholesterol	0.84 mg
Energy (kcals/kj)	94/394

1 Boil the potatoes until soft enough to be mashed. Mash these down using a masher.

2 ▲ Blend together the remaining ingredients in a small bowl.

3 ▲ Stir the mixture into the mashed potatoes and mix together thoroughly with a fork.

4 Serve warm as an accompaniment.

Spicy Cabbage

An excellent vegetable accompaniment, this is very versatile and can be served even as a warm side salad.

SERVES 4

INGREDIENTS
50 g/2 oz/4 tbsp low-fat margarine
1/2 tsp white cumin seeds
3–8 dried red chillies, to taste
1 small onion, sliced
225 g/8 oz/2 1/2 cups cabbage, shredded
2 medium carrots, grated
1/2 tsp salt
2 tbsp lemon juice

NUTRITIONAL VALUES (per portion)	
Total fat	6.06 g
Saturated fat	1.28 g
Cholesterol	0.84 mg
Energy (kcals/kj)	92/384

2 ▲ Add the sliced onion and fry for about 2 minutes. Add the cabbage and carrots and stir-fry for a further 5 minutes or until the cabbage is soft.

3 Finally, stir in the salt and lemon juice and serve.

1 ▲ Melt the low-fat margarine in a medium saucepan and fry the white cumin seeds and dried red chillies for about 30 seconds.

Masala Mashed Potatoes (top) and Spicy Cabbage

Spiced Potatoes and Carrots Parisienne

Ready prepared "parisienne" vegetables have recently become available in many supermarkets. These are simply root vegetables that have been peeled and cut into perfectly spherical shapes. This dish looks extremely fresh and appetizing and is equally delicious.

SERVES 4

INGREDIENTS
175 g/6 oz carrots parisienne
175 g/6 oz potatoes parisienne
115 g/4 oz runner beans, sliced
75 g/3 oz/6 tbsp butter
1 tbsp corn oil
1/4 tsp onion seeds
1/4 tsp fenugreek seeds
4 dried red chillies
1/2 tsp mustard seeds
6 curry leaves
1 medium onion, sliced
1 tsp salt
4 garlic cloves, sliced
4 fresh red chillies
1 tbsp chopped fresh coriander (cilantro)
1 tbsp chopped fresh mint
mint sprig

1 ▲ Drop the carrots, potatoes and runner beans into a pan of boiling water, and cook for about 7 minutes, or until they are just tender but not overcooked. Drain and set to one side.

2 ▲ Heat the butter and oil in a deep round-bottomed frying pan (skillet) or a large karahi and add the onion seeds, fenugreek seeds, dried red chillies, mustard seeds and curry leaves. When these have sizzled for a few seconds, add the onion and fry for 3–5 minutes.

3 ▲ Add the salt, garlic and fresh chillies, followed by the cooked vegetables, and stir gently for about 5 minutes, over a medium heat.

4 Add the fresh coriander (cilantro) and mint and serve hot garnished with a sprig of mint.

Karahi Shredded Cabbage with Cumin

This cabbage dish is only lightly spiced and makes a good accompaniment to most other dishes.

SERVES 4

INGREDIENTS
1 tbsp corn oil
50 g/2 oz/4 tbsp butter
½ tsp crushed coriander seeds
½ tsp white cumin seeds
6 dried red chillies
1 small savoy cabbage, shredded
12 mange-tout (snow peas)
3 fresh red chillies, seeded and sliced
12 baby corn cobs
salt, to taste
25 g/1 oz/¼ cup flaked (slivered)
*   almonds, toasted*
1 tbsp chopped fresh coriander (cilantro)

1 Heat the oil and butter in a deep round-bottomed frying pan (skillet) or a karahi and add the crushed coriander seeds, white cumin seeds and dried red chillies.

2 ▲ Add the shredded cabbage and mange-tout (snow peas) and stir-fry for about 5 minutes.

3 ▲ Finally add the fresh red chillies, baby corn cobs and salt, and fry for a further 3 minutes.

4 Garnish with the toasted almonds and fresh coriander (cilantro), and serve hot.

Potatoes in a Hot Red Sauce

This dish should be hot and sour but, if you wish, reduce the chillies and add extra tomato purée (paste) instead.

SERVES 4–6

INGREDIENTS
450 g/1 lb small new potatoes
25 g/1 oz dried red chillies, preferably kashmiri
1½ tsp cumin seeds
4 cloves garlic
6 tbsp vegetable oil
4 tbsp thick tamarind juice
2 tbsp tomato purée (paste)
4 curry leaves
salt, to taste
1 tsp sugar
¼ tsp asafoetida
coriander (cilantro) sprig, to garnish

1 ▲ Boil the potatoes until they are fully cooked, ensuring they do not break. To test, insert a thin sharp knife into the potatoes. It should come out clean when the potatoes are fully cooked. Drain well.

2 Soak the chillies for 5 minutes in warm water. Drain and grind with the cumin seeds and garlic to a coarse paste using a pestle and mortar or food processor.

3 ▲ Heat the oil in a frying pan (skillet). Fry the paste, tamarind juice, tomato purée (paste), curry leaves, salt, sugar and asafoetida until the oil separates. Add the potatoes. Reduce the heat, cover and simmer for about 5 minutes. Garnish and serve.

Cucumber Curry

This makes a pleasant accompaniment to fish dishes and may be served cold with cooked meats.

SERVES 4–6

INGREDIENTS
120 ml/4 fl oz/½ cup water
115 g/4 oz creamed coconut
½ tsp turmeric
salt, to taste
1 tsp sugar
1 large cucumber, cut into small pieces
1 large red (bell) pepper, cut into small pieces
50 g/2 oz salted peanuts, coarsely crushed
4 tbsp vegetable oil
2 dried red chillies
1 tsp cumin seeds
1 tsp mustard seeds
4–6 curry leaves
4 cloves garlic, crushed
a few whole salted peanuts, to garnish

1 ▲ Bring the water to the boil in a heavy pan and add the creamed coconut, turmeric, salt and sugar. Simmer until the coconut dissolves to obtain smooth, thick sauce.

2 Add the cucumber, red (bell) pepper and crushed peanuts and simmer for about 5 minutes. Transfer to a heatproof serving dish and keep warm.

3 ▲ Heat the oil in a frying pan (skillet). Fry the chillies and cumin with the mustard seeds until they start to pop. Reduce the heat, add the curry leaves and garlic and fry. Pour over the cucumber mixture and stir well. Garnish and serve hot.

Potatoes in a Hot Red Sauce (top) and Cucumber Curry

Sweet-and-Sour Vegetables with Paneer

LOW-FAT RECIPE

This is one of my favourite grilled (broiled) vegetable selections. The cheese used in this recipe is Indian paneer, which can be bought at some Asian stores; tofu can be used in its place.

SERVES 4

INGREDIENTS

1 green pepper, cut into squares
1 yellow pepper, cut into squares
8 cherry, or 4 salad, tomatoes
8 cauliflower florets (flowerets)
8 pineapple chunks
8 cubes paneer (see Introduction)

Seasoned oil
1 tbsp soya oil
2 tbsp lemon juice
1 tsp salt
1 tsp crushed black peppercorns
1 tbsp clear honey
2 tbsp chilli sauce

NUTRITIONAL VALUES (per portion)	
Total fat	9.80 g
Saturated fat	4.43 g
Cholesterol	20.00 mg
Energy (kcals/kj)	171/718

1 ▲ Preheat the grill (broiler) to hot. Thread the prepared vegetables, pineapple and the paneer onto 4 skewers, alternating the ingredients. Set the skewers on a flameproof dish or grill tray.

2 In a small mixing bowl, mix all the ingredients for the seasoned oil. If the mixture is a little too thick, add 1 tbsp of water to loosen it.

3 ▲ Using a pastry brush, baste the vegetables with the seasoned oil. Grill (broil) under the preheated grill for about 10 minutes until the vegetables begin to darken slightly, turning the skewers to cook evenly.

4 Serve on a bed of plain boiled rice.

Vegetables and Beans with Curry Leaves

LOW-FAT RECIPE

Fresh curry leaves are extremely aromatic and there is no substitute for them. Fresh curry leaves also freeze well, but if necessary you can use dried ones. This is quite a dry curry.

SERVES 4

INGREDIENTS

2 tbsp vegetable oil
6 curry leaves
3 garlic cloves, sliced
3 dried red chillies
1/4 tsp onion seeds
1/4 tsp fenugreek seeds
3 fresh green chillies, chopped
2 tsp desiccated (shredded) coconut
115 g/4 oz/1/2 cup canned red kidney beans, drained

1 medium carrot, cut into strips
50 g/2 oz French beans, diagonally sliced
1 medium red (bell) pepper, cut into strips
1 tsp salt
2 tbsp lemon juice

NUTRITIONAL VALUES (per portion)	
Total fat	8.27 g
Saturated fat	2.47 g
Cholesterol	0.00 mg
Energy (kcals/kj)	130/548

1 Heat the oil in a medium deep frying pan (skillet). Add the curry leaves, garlic cloves, dried chillies, and onion and fenugreek seeds.

2 ▲ When these turn a shade darker, add the remaining ingredients, stirring constantly. Lower the heat, cover and cook for about 5 minutes.

3 Transfer to a serving dish and serve with extra coconut, if wished.

Sweet-and-Sour Vegetables with Paneer (top) and Vegetables and Beans with Curry Leaves

Corn Cob Curry

Corn-cobs are roasted on charcoal and rubbed with lemon juice, salt and chilli powder in India. In season, vendors fill the atmosphere with these delicious aromas. Corn is also a popular curry ingredient.

SERVES 4–6

INGREDIENTS
4 whole corn-cobs, fresh, canned or frozen
vegetable oil, for frying
1 large onion, finely chopped
2 cloves garlic, crushed
1 piece fresh ginger, 5 cm/2 in long,
    crushed
1/2 tsp turmeric
1/2 tsp onion seeds
1/2 tsp cumin seeds
1/2 tsp five-spice powder
chilli powder, to taste
6–8 curry leaves
1/2 tsp sugar
200 ml/7 fl oz/scant 1 cup natural (plain)
    yogurt

1 ▲ Cut each corn-cob in half, using a sharp, heavy knife or cleaver to make clean cuts and prevent damaging the kernels. Heat the oil in a large frying pan (skillet) and fry the corn pieces until golden brown on all sides. Remove the corn-cobs and set aside.

2 ▲ Remove any excess oil leaving about 2 tbsp in the pan. Grind the onion, garlic and ginger to a paste using a pestle and mortar or food processor. Remove and mix in all the spices, curry leaves and sugar.

3 ▲ Reheat the oil gently and fry the onion mixture until all the spices have blended well and the oil separates from the paste.

4 ▲ Cool the mixture and gradually fold in the yogurt. Mix well until you have a smooth sauce. Add the corn to the mixture and mix well so all the pieces are evenly covered with the sauce. Gently reheat for about 10 minutes. Serve hot.

Curried Stuffed (Bell) Peppers

This is one of the most famous dishes of Deccan. Hot, spicy and extremely delicious, it is often prepared for weddings. It is made with extra oil several days in advance to allow the spices to mature.

SERVES 4–6

INGREDIENTS

1 tbsp sesame seeds
1 tbsp white poppy seeds
1 tsp coriander seeds
4 tbsp desiccated (shredded) coconut
1/2 onion, sliced
1 piece fresh ginger, 2.5 cm/1 in long, sliced
4 cloves garlic, sliced
handful of fresh coriander (cilantro)
2 fresh green chillies
4 tbsp vegetable oil
2 potatoes, boiled and coarsely mashed
salt, to taste
2 each, green, red and yellow (bell) peppers
2 tbsp sesame oil
1 tsp cumin seeds
4 fresh green chillies, slit
4 tbsp tamarind juice

2 ▲ Heat 2 tbsp of the vegetable oil in a frying pan and fry the ground paste for 4–5 minutes. Add the potatoes and salt and stir well until the spices have blended evenly into the potatoes.

3 ▲ Trim the bases of the peppers so they stand, then slice off the tops and reserve. Remove the seeds and any white pith. Fill the peppers with equal amounts of the potato mixture and replace the tops.

4 ▲ Heat the sesame oil and remaining vegetable oil in a frying pan and fry the cumin seeds and the slit green chillies. When the chillies turn white, add the tamarind juice and bring to the boil. Place the peppers over the mixture, cover the pan and cook until the peppers are nearly done.

1 ▲ In a frying pan (skillet), dry-fry the sesame, poppy and coriander seeds, then add the desiccated (shredded) coconut and continue to roast until the coconut turns golden brown. Add the onion, ginger, garlic, coriander (cilantro), and chillies and roast for a further 5 minutes. Cool, and grind to a paste using a pestle and mortar or food processor. Put aside.

Spicy Balti Potatoes

SERVES 4

INGREDIENTS

3 tbsp corn oil
½ tsp white cumin seeds
3 curry leaves
1 tsp crushed dried red chillies
½ tsp mixed onion, mustard and
*   fenugreek seeds*
½ tsp fennel seeds
3 garlic cloves
½ tsp shredded ginger
2 medium onions, sliced
6 new potatoes, cut into 5 mm/¼ in slices
1 tbsp chopped fresh coriander (cilantro)
1 fresh red chilli, seeded and sliced
1 fresh green chilli, seeded and sliced

1 ▲ Heat the oil in a deep round-bottomed frying pan (skillet) or a karahi. Lower the heat slightly and add the cumin seeds, curry leaves, dried red chillies, mixed onion, mustard and fenugreek seeds, fennel seeds, garlic cloves and ginger. Fry for about 1 minute, then add the onions and fry for 5 minutes or until the onions are golden brown.

2 ▲ Add the potatoes, fresh coriander (cilantro) and fresh red and green chillies and mix well. Cover the pan tightly with a lid or foil, making sure the foil does not touch the food. Cook over a very low heat for about 7 minutes or until the potatoes are tender.

3 Remove the foil and serve hot.

Okra with Green Mango and Lentils

If you like okra, you'll love this spicy and tangy dish.

SERVES 4

INGREDIENTS

115 g/4 oz/⅔ cup yellow lentils (toor
*   dhal)*
3 tbsp corn oil
½ tsp onion seeds
2 medium onions, sliced
½ tsp ground fenugreek
1 tsp ginger pulp
1 tsp garlic pulp
1½ tsp chilli powder
¼ tsp turmeric
1 tsp ground coriander
1 green (unripe) mango, peeled and sliced
450 g/1 lb okra, cut into 1 cm/½ in pieces
1½ tsp salt
2 fresh red chillies, seeded and sliced
2 tbsp chopped fresh coriander (cilantro)
1 tomato, sliced

1 ▲ Wash the lentils thoroughly and put in a saucepan with enough water to cover. Bring to the boil and cook until soft but not mushy. Drain and set to one side.

2 Heat the oil in a deep round-bottomed frying pan (skillet) or a karahi and fry the onion seeds until they begin to pop. Add the onions and fry until golden brown. Lower the heat and add the ground fenugreek, ginger, garlic, chilli powder, turmeric and ground coriander.

3 ▲ Throw in the mango slices and the okra. Stir well and add the salt, red chillies and fresh coriander (cilantro). Stir-fry for about 3 minutes or until the okra is well cooked.

4 Finally, add the cooked lentils and sliced tomato and cook for a further 3 minutes. Serve hot.

Spicy Balti Potatoes (top) and Okra with Green Mango and Lentils

Masala Beans with Fenugreek

LOW-FAT RECIPE

"Masala" means spice and this vegetarian dish is spicy, though not necessarily hot.

SERVES 4

INGREDIENTS
1 medium onion
1 tsp ground cumin
1 tsp ground coriander
1 tsp sesame seeds
1 tsp chilli powder
½ tsp garlic pulp
¼ tsp turmeric
1 tsp salt
2 tbsp vegetable oil
1 tomato, quartered
225 g/8 oz French (green) beans
1 bunch fresh fenugreek leaves, stems discarded
4 tbsp chopped fresh coriander (cilantro)
1 tbsp lemon juice

NUTRITIONAL VALUES (per portion)	
Total fat	7.11 g
Saturated fat	0.88 g
Cholesterol	0.00 mg
Energy (kcals/kj)	100/419

1 Roughly chop the onion. Mix together the ground cumin and coriander, sesame seeds, chilli powder, garlic, turmeric and salt.

2 ▲ Place all of these ingredients, including the onion, in a food processor and process for 30–45 seconds.

3 ▲ In a medium saucepan, heat the oil and fry the spice mixture for about 5 minutes, stirring occasionally.

4 ▲ Add the tomato, French (green) beans, fresh fenugreek and fresh coriander (cilantro).

5 ▲ Stir-fry for about 5 minutes, sprinkle in the lemon juice and serve.

Vegetables with Almonds

Natural (plain) yogurt is added to the vegetables towards the end of the cooking time, which not only gives this dish a tangy note but also makes it creamy.

SERVES 4

INGREDIENTS
2 tbsp vegetable oil
2 medium onions, sliced
5 cm/2 in piece fresh ginger, shredded
1 tsp crushed black peppercorns
1 bay leaf
¼ tsp turmeric
1 tsp ground coriander
1 tsp salt
½ tsp garam masala
175 g/6 oz/2½ cups mushrooms, thickly
    sliced
1 medium courgette (zucchini), thickly
    sliced
50 g/2 oz French beans, sliced into
    2.5 cm/1 in pieces
1 tbsp roughly chopped fresh mint
150 ml/¼ pint/⅔ cup water
2 tbsp natural (plain) low-fat yogurt
25 g/1 oz/¼ cup flaked (slivered) almonds

NUTRITIONAL VALUES (per portion)	
Total fat	10.11 g
Saturated fat	1.14 g
Cholesterol	0.30 mg
Energy (kcals/kj)	136/569

2 ▲ Lower the heat and add the turmeric, ground coriander, salt and garam masala, stirring occasionally. Gradually add the mushrooms, courgette (zucchini), French beans and the mint. Stir gently so that the vegetables retain their shapes.

3 Pour in the water and bring to a simmer, then lower the heat and cook until the water has been absorbed by the vegetables.

4 ▲ Beat the yogurt with a fork, then pour onto the vegetables and mix together well.

5 Cook for a further 2–3 minutes, stirring occasionally. Serve garnished with the flaked (slivered) almonds.

1 ▲ In a medium deep frying pan (skillet), heat the oil and fry the sliced onions with the shredded ginger, crushed black peppercorns and bay leaf for 3–5 minutes.

Pulses

Widely eaten in India, spicy pulses are both nutritious and tasty. Even everyday pulses, such as lentils and black-eyed beans, are transformed into delectable dishes by flavouring with blends of spices, and chick-peas are often curried to serve with tasty potato cakes. Less familiar pulses are worth searching for — Black Gram in a Spicy Cream Sauce is particularly tasty.

Lentils Seasoned with Fried Spices

Dhal is cooked in every house in India in one form or another. This recipe is a simplified version.

SERVES 4–6

INGREDIENTS
115 g/4 oz/¹/₂ cup red gram
50 g/2 oz/¹/₄ cup bengal gram
350 ml/12 fl oz/1¹/₂ cups water
4 fresh green chillies
1 tsp turmeric
1 large onion, sliced
salt, to taste
400 g/14 oz canned plum tomatoes, crushed
4 tbsp vegetable oil
¹/₂ tsp mustard seeds
¹/₂ tsp cumin seeds
1 clove garlic, crushed
6 curry leaves
2 dried red chillies
¹/₄ tsp asafoetida
deep-fried onions and fresh coriander (cilantro), to garnish

1 ▲ Place the first 6 ingredients in a heavy pan and bring to the boil. Simmer, covered, until the lentils are soft and the water has evaporated.

2 ▲ Mash the lentils with the back of a spoon. When nearly smooth, add the salt and tomatoes and mix well. If necessary, thin the mixture with hot water.

3 Fry the remaining ingredients until the garlic browns. Pour the oil and spices over the lentils and cover. After 5 minutes, mix well, garnish, and serve.

South Indian Lentils and Vegetables

Sambhar is a favourite south Indian dish served for breakfast with dosai (Indian pancakes) or idli (rice dumplings).

SERVES 4–6

INGREDIENTS
4 tbsp vegetable oil
¹/₂ tsp mustard seeds
¹/₂ tsp cumin seeds
2 dried red chillies
¹/₄ tsp asafoetida
6–8 curry leaves
2 cloves garlic, crushed
2 tbsp desiccated (shredded) coconut
225 g/8 oz/1 cup split red lentils (masoor dhal)
2 tsp sambhar masala
¹/₂ tsp turmeric
450 ml/³/₄ pint/scant 2 cups water
450 g/1 lb mixed vegetables, eg okra, courgettes (zucchini), cauliflower, shallots and (bell) peppers
4 tbsp tamarind juice
4 firm tomatoes, quartered
4 tbsp vegetable oil
2 cloves garlic, finely sliced
handful fresh coriander (cilantro), chopped

1 ▲ Heat the oil in a heavy saucepan. Fry the next 7 ingredients until the coconut browns. Mix in the lentils, sambhar masala, turmeric and water.

2 Simmer until the lentils are mushy. Add the vegetables, tamarind juice and tomatoes. Cook so the vegetables are crunchy.

3 ▲ Fry the garlic slices and fresh coriander (cilantro). Pour over the lentils and vegetables. Mix at the table before serving.

Lentils Seasoned with Fried Spices (top) and South Indian Lentils and Vegetables

Curried Chick-Peas (Garbanzos) with Potato Cakes

*N*o other city in India is quite like Bombay. Its cuisine is typical of food you can buy right off the streets, which is the way the Bombayites like it – spicy, quick and nutritious.

SERVES 4–6

INGREDIENTS
2 tbsp vegetable oil
2 tbsp ground coriander
2 tbsp ground cumin
¹/₂ tsp turmeric
¹/₂ tsp salt
¹/₂ tsp sugar
2 tbsp flour paste
450 g/1 lb chick-peas (garbanzos), cooked and drained
2 fresh green chillies, chopped
1 piece fresh ginger, 5 cm/2 in long, finely crushed
75 g/3 oz/3 cups fresh coriander (cilantro), chopped
2 firm tomatoes, chopped

Potato Cakes
450 g/1 lb potatoes, boiled and coarsely mashed
4 fresh green chillies, finely chopped
50 g/2 oz/2 cups fresh coriander (cilantro), finely chopped
1¹/₂ tsp cumin powder
1 tsp mango powder
salt, to taste
vegetable oil, for shallow-frying

1 ▲ For the curry, heat the oil in a large saucepan and fry the coriander, cumin, turmeric, salt, sugar and flour paste, stirring frequently, until the water has evaporated and the oil separated out from the mixture.

2 ▲ Add the chick-peas (garbanzos), chillies, ginger, fresh coriander (cilantro) and tomatoes. Toss well and simmer for about 5 minutes. Remove to a serving dish and keep warm.

3 ▲ To make the potato cakes, in a large mixing bowl mix the mashed potato with the green chillies, ground coriander and cumin, mango powder and salt. Mix until all the ingredients are well blended.

4 ▲ Using your hands, shape the potato mixture into little cakes. Heat the oil in a shallow frying pan (skillet) or griddle and fry the cakes on both sides until golden brown. Transfer to a serving dish and serve with the curried chick-peas.

Black Gram in a Spicy Cream Sauce

Dhabas – highway cafes – are very lively eating places serving a variety of dishes. This recipe is commonly served, and is one of the most popular.

SERVES 4–6

INGREDIENTS

175 g/6 oz/²/₃ cup black gram (urid dhal), soaked overnight
50 g/2 oz/¹/₄ cup red gram
120ml/4 fl oz/¹/₂ cup double (heavy) cream
120 ml/4 fl oz/¹/₂ cup natural (plain) yogurt
1 tsp cornflour (cornstarch)
3 tbsp ghee
1 onion, finely chopped
1 piece fresh ginger, 5 cm/2 in long, crushed
4 fresh green chillies, chopped
1 tomato, chopped
¹/₂ tsp chilli powder
¹/₂ tsp turmeric
¹/₂ tsp ground cumin
salt, to taste
2 cloves garlic, sliced

1 ▲ Drain the black gram and place in a heavy pan with the red gram. Cover with water and bring to the boil. Reduce the heat, cover the pan and simmer until the gram are tender. The black gram will remain whole but the red gram will be mushy. Gently mash with a spoon. Allow to cool.

2 ▲ In a bowl, mix together the cream, yogurt and cornflour (cornstarch). Mix the cream mixture into the gram without damaging the whole black gram grains.

3 ▲ Heat 1 tbsp of the ghee in a frying pan (skillet) and fry the onion, ginger, 2 of the green chillies and the tomato until the onion is soft. Add the spices and salt and fry for a further 2 minutes. Add it all to the gram mixture and mix well. Reheat and transfer to a heatproof serving dish and keep warm.

4 ▲ Heat the remaining ghee in a frying pan and fry the garlic slices and remaining chillies until the garlic slices are golden brown. Pour over the gram and serve, folding the garlic and chilli into the gram just before serving.

Black-Eyed Peas and Potato Curry

Black-eyed peas are beige and kidney-shaped with a distinctive dark dot. This can be served as an appetizer or snack.

SERVES 4–6

INGREDIENTS
225 g/8 oz/1⅓ cups black-eyed peas, soaked overnight and drained
¼ tsp bicarbonate of soda (baking soda)
1 tsp five-spice powder
¼ tsp asafoetida
2 onions, finely chopped
1 piece fresh ginger, 2.5 cm/1 in long, crushed
few fresh mint leaves
450 ml/¾ pint/scant 1½ cups water
4 tbsp vegetable oil
½ tsp each, turmeric, ground coriander, ground cumin and chilli powder
4 fresh green chillies, chopped

75 ml/5 tbsp tamarind juice
2 potatoes, cubed and boiled
115 g/4 oz/4 cups fresh coriander (cilantro), chopped
2 firm tomatoes, chopped
salt, to taste

1 ▲ Place the black-eyed peas with the first 7 ingredients in a heavy pan. Simmer until the beans are soft. Remove any excess water and reserve.

2 ▲ Heat the oil in a frying pan (skillet). Gently fry the spices, chillies and tamarind juice, until they are well blended. Pour over the black-eyed peas and mix.

3 Add the potatoes, fresh coriander (cilantro), tomatoes and salt. Mix well, and if necessary add a little reserved water. Reheat and serve.

Bengal Gram and Bottle Gourd Curry

This is an Anglo-Indian version of dhal, which is characteristically hot, and with the dhals left whole.

SERVES 4–6

INGREDIENTS
175 g/6 oz/⅔ cup bengal gram
450 ml/¾ pint/1½ cups water
4 tbsp vegetable oil
2 fresh green chillies, chopped
1 onion, chopped
2 cloves garlic, crushed
1 piece fresh ginger, 5 cm/2 in long, crushed
6–8 curry leaves
1 tsp chilli powder
1 tsp turmeric
salt, to taste
450 g/1 lb bottle gourd or marrow (squash), courgettes (zucchini) or pumpkin, peeled, pithed and sliced

4 tbsp tamarind juice
2 tomatoes, chopped
handful fresh coriander (cilantro), chopped

1 ▲ In a saucepan, cook the lentils in the water until the grains are tender but not mushy. Put aside without draining away any excess water.

2 ▲ Heat the oil in a deep saucepan. Fry the chillies, onion, garlic, ginger, curry leaves, chilli powder, turmeric and salt. Add the gourd pieces and mix. Cover and cook until the gourd is soft.

3 Add the lentils and water and bring to the boil. Add the tamarind juice, tomatoes and fresh coriander (cilantro). Simmer gently until the gourd is cooked. Serve hot with a dry meat curry.

Black-Eyed Peas and Potato Curry (top) and Bengal Gram and Bottle Gourd Curry

Green Gram and Rice

The whole spices are edible, but it is advisable to warn the diners about them.

SERVES 4–6

INGREDIENTS
4 tbsp ghee
1 onion, finely chopped
2 cloves garlic, crushed
1 piece ginger, 2.5 cm/1 in long, shredded
4 fresh green chillies, chopped
4 cloves
1 piece cinnamon stick, 2.5 cm/1 in long
4 green cardamom pods
1 tsp turmeric
salt, to taste
350 g/12 oz/1¾ cups patna rice, washed and soaked for 20 minutes

175 g/6 oz/⅔ cup split green gram, washed and soaked for 20 minutes
600 ml/1 pint/2½ cups water

1 ▲ Gently heat the ghee in a large heavy pan with a tight-fitting cover and fry the onion, garlic, ginger, chillies, cloves, cinnamon, cardamoms, turmeric and salt until the onion is soft and translucent.

2 ▲ Drain the rice and gram, add to the spices and sauté for 2–3 minutes. Add the water and bring to the boil. Reduce the heat, cover and cook for about 20–25 minutes or until all the water is absorbed.

3 Take the pan off the heat and leave to rest for 5 minutes. Just before serving gently toss the mixture with a flat spatula.

Split Lentils with Courgettes (Zucchini)

Most dhal dishes are runny but this one provides texture with the addition of the courgettes (zucchini).

SERVES 4–6

INGREDIENTS
175 g/6 oz/⅔ cup small split yellow lentils (moong dhal)
½ tsp turmeric
300 ml/½ pint/1¼ cups water
4 tbsp vegetable oil
1 large onion, finely sliced
2 cloves garlic, crushed
2 fresh green chillies, chopped
½ tsp mustard seeds
½ tsp cumin seeds
¼ tsp asafoetida
few fresh coriander (cilantro) and mint leaves, chopped
6–8 curry leaves
salt, to taste
½ tsp sugar
200 g/7 oz canned tomatoes, chopped

225 g/8 oz courgettes (zucchini), cut into small pieces
4 tbsp lemon juice

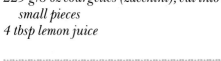

1 ▲ In a saucepan, boil the lentils and turmeric in the water and then simmer until the dhal is cooked but not mushy. Drain and reserve both the liquid and the dhal.

2 ▲ Heat the oil in a frying pan (skillet) and fry the remaining ingredients except the lemon juice. Cover and cook until the courgettes (zucchini) are nearly tender but still crunchy.

3 Fold in the drained dhal and the lemon juice. If the dish is too dry, add a small amount of the reserved water. Reheat and serve.

Green Gram and Rice (top) and Split Lentils with Courgettes (Zucchini)

Tarka Dhal

Tarka dhal is probably the most popular of lentil dishes and is found in most Indian/Pakistani restaurants.

SERVES 4

INGREDIENTS
115 g/4 oz/½ cup masoor dhal (split red lentils)
50 g/2 oz/¼ cup moong dhal (small split yellow lentils)
600 ml/1 pint/2½ cups water
1 tsp ginger pulp
1 tsp garlic pulp
¼ tsp turmeric
2 fresh green chillies, chopped
1½ tsp salt

Tarka
2 tbsp vegetable oil
1 onion, sliced
¼ tsp mixed mustard and onion seeds
4 dried red chillies
1 tomato, sliced

Garnish
1 tbsp chopped fresh coriander (cilantro)
1–2 fresh green chillies, seeded and sliced
1 tbsp chopped fresh mint

NUTRITIONAL VALUES (per portion)

Total fat	6.61 g
Saturated fat	0.90 g
Cholesterol	0.00 mg
Energy (kcals/kj)	179/752

1 Pick over the lentils for any stones before washing them.

2 ▲ Boil the lentils in the water with the ginger, garlic, turmeric and chopped green chillies for 15–20 minutes or until soft.

3 ▲ Mash the lentil mixture down. The consistency of the mashed lentils should be similar to a creamy chicken soup.

4 ▲ If the mixture looks too dry, add more water. Season with the salt.

5 ▲ To prepare the tarka, heat the oil and fry the onion with the mustard and onion seeds, dried red chillies and sliced tomato for 2 minutes.

6 ▲ Pour the tarka over the dhal and garnish with fresh coriander (cilantro), green chillies and mint.

COOK'S TIP

Dried red chillies are available in many different sizes. If the ones you have are large, or if you want a less spicy flavour, reduce the quantity specified to 1–2.

Breads & Rice Dishes

Indian dishes are often served with breads and you'll find that Naan, Chapati and the deliciously flaky Paratha are surprisingly easy to make at home. Rice can be as plain or as exotic as you like – simply boiled, delicately spiced, or mixed with refreshing fruits as an accompaniment. It can also be layered with chicken and potatoes to make a tasty main meal.

Plain Boiled Rice

In India, rice is consumed in great quantities by all members of society. There are numerous ways in which it can be prepared, but plain boiled rice is the most common.

SERVES 4–6

INGREDIENTS
1 tbsp ghee, unsalted (sweet) butter or olive oil
350 g/12 oz/1¾ cups basmati rice, washed and drained
450 ml/¾ pint/scant 2 cups water
salt, to taste

1 ▲ Heat the ghee, butter or oil in a saucepan and sauté the drained rice thoroughly for about 2–3 minutes.

COOK'S TIP

To make a fragrantly spiced version, sauté 4–6 green cardamom pods, 4 cloves, 5 cm/2 in piece cinnamon stick, ½ tsp black cumin seeds and 2 bay leaves. Add 350 g/

2 ▲ Add the water and salt and bring to the boil. Reduce the heat to low, cover and cook gently for 15–20 minutes. To serve, fluff the grains gently with a fork.

12 oz/1¾ cups drained basmati rice and proceed as for plain boiled rice. For an even more luxurious rice, add 6–8 strands of saffron and sauté with the spices.

Fragrant Meat Pullao

This rice dish acquires its delicious taste not only from the spices but the richly flavoured meat stock.

SERVES 4–6

INGREDIENTS
900 g/2 lb chicken pieces, or lean lamb, cubed
600 ml/1 pint/2½ cups water
4 green cardamom pods
2 black cardamom pods
10 black peppercorns
4 cloves
1 medium onion, sliced
salt, to taste
450 g/1 lb/2¼ cups basmati rice, washed and drained
8–10 saffron strands
2 cloves garlic, crushed
1 piece fresh ginger, 5 cm/2 in long, crushed

1 piece cinnamon stick, 5 cm/2 in long
175 g/6 oz/1 cup sultanas (golden raisins) and blanched almonds, sautéed, to garnish

1 ▲ In a large saucepan, cook the chicken or lamb in the water with the cardamom pods, peppercorns, cloves, onion and salt until the meat is cooked. Remove the meat with a slotted spoon and keep warm. Strain the stock if you wish, and return to the saucepan.

2 ▼ Add the rice, saffron, garlic, ginger and cinnamon to the stock and bring the contents to the boil.

3 Quickly add the meat and stir well. Bring back to the boil, reduce the heat and cover. Cook covered for about 15–20 minutes. Remove from the heat and leave to stand for 5 minutes. Garnish with sultanas (golden raisins) and almonds and serve.

Plain Boiled Rice (top) and Fragrant Meat Pullao

Saffron and Cardamom Flavoured Rice

LOW-FAT RECIPE

There are two main ways of cooking rice: one is total absorption of water and the other is where you drain the water, which gets rid of any starch from the rice. For this recipe I have chosen the latter for obvious reasons.

SERVES 6

INGREDIENTS
450 g/1 lb/2¼ cups basmati rice
750 ml/1¼ pints/good 3 cups water
3 green cardamom pods
2 cloves
1 tsp salt
½ tsp crushed saffron strands
3 tbsp semi-skimmed (2%) milk

NUTRITIONAL VALUES (per portion)

Total fat	0.79 g
Saturated fat	0.19 g
Cholesterol	1.31 mg
Energy (kcals/kj)	264/1108

1 ▲ Wash the rice at least twice and place it in a medium saucepan with the water.

2 ▲ Toss all the whole spices into the saucepan along with the salt. Bring to the boil, cover and simmer for about 10 minutes.

3 Meanwhile, place the saffron and semi-skimmed (2%) milk in a small pan and warm. Alternatively, put the ingredients in a cup and warm for 1 minute in the microwave.

4 ▲ Now return to the rice to see if it is fully cooked. Use a slotted spoon to lift out a few grains and press the rice between your index finger and thumb. It should feel soft on the outside but still a little hard in the middle.

5 Remove the pan from the heat and carefully drain the rice through a sieve (strainer).

6 ▲ Transfer the rice back into the pan and pour the saffron and milk over the top of the rice.

7 ▲ Cover with a tight-fitting lid and place the pan back on a medium heat for 7–10 minutes.

8 After cooking, remove the pan from the heat and leave the rice to stand for a further 5 minutes before serving.

COOK'S TIP

Basmati rice is unequalled in flavour and texture and is the best variety to choose for Indian rice dishes. It is available from large supermarkets and Asian stores.

Rice Layered with Lentils

Bhori Muslims in India have their own special style of cooking and have adapted many of the traditional dishes from other Indian communities. This rice and lentil dish is served with a gourd curry, or Palida, which is prominently flavoured with fenugreek and soured with dried mangosteen (kokum). Lemon juice will provide the same effect.

SERVES 4–6

INGREDIENTS

175 g/6 oz/²⁄₃ cup bengal gram
600 ml/1 pint/2¹⁄₂ cups water
¹⁄₂ tsp turmeric
50 g/2 oz deep-fried onions, crushed
3 tbsp green masala paste
few fresh mint and coriander leaves, chopped
salt, to taste
350 g/12 oz/1³⁄₄ cups basmati rice, cooked
2 tbsp ghee
a little water

Curry

4 tbsp vegetable oil
¹⁄₄ tsp fenugreek seeds
15 g/¹⁄₂ oz dried fenugreek leaves
2 cloves garlic, crushed
1 tsp ground coriander
1 tsp cumin seeds
1 tsp chilli powder
4 tbsp gram flour mixed with 4 tbsp water
450 g/1 lb bottle gourd, peeled, pith and seeds removed and cut into bite-size pieces, or marrow (squash) or firm courgettes (zucchini) prepared in same way
175 ml/6 fl oz/³⁄₄ cup tomato juice
6 dried mangosteen (kokum), or juice of 3 lemons
salt, to taste

1 ▲ For the rice, boil the bengal gram in the water with the turmeric until the grains are soft but not mushy. Drain and reserve the water for the curry.

2 ▲ Toss the bengal gram gently with the deep-fried onions, green masala paste, chopped fresh mint and coriander, and salt.

3 ▲ Grease a heavy pan and place a layer of rice in the bottom. Add the bengal gram mixture and another layer of the remaining rice. Place small knobs of ghee on top, sprinkle with a little water and gently heat until steam gathers in the pan.

4 ▲ To make the curry, heat the oil in a pan and fry the fenugreek seeds and leaves and garlic until the garlic turns golden brown.

5 ▲ Mix the ground coriander, cumin and chilli powder to a paste with a little water. Add to the pan and simmer until all the water evaporates.

6 ▲ Add the remaining ingredients, and cook until the gourd is soft and transparent. Serve hot with the rice.

Colourful Pullao Rice

*This lightly spiced rice makes an
extremely attractive accompaniment to
many Balti dishes, and is easily made.*

SERVES 4–6

INGREDIENTS
*450 g/1 lb/2⅓ cups basmati rice
75 g/3 oz/6 tbsp unsalted butter
4 cloves
4 green cardamom pods
1 bay leaf
1 tsp salt
1 litre/1¾ pints/4 cups water
a few drops each of yellow, green and red
    food colouring*

1 Wash the rice twice, drain and set
aside in a sieve (strainer).

2 ▲ Melt the butter in a medium
saucepan, and throw in the cloves,
cardamoms, bay leaf and salt. Lower
the heat and add the rice. Fry for about
1 minute, stirring constantly.

3 Add the water and bring to the boil.
As soon as it has boiled, cover the pan
and reduce the heat. Cook for 15–20
minutes.

4 ▲ Just before you are ready to serve
the rice, pour a few drops of each
colouring at different sides of the pan.
Leave to stand for 5 minutes, mix
gently and serve.

Fruity Pullao

SERVES 4–6

INGREDIENTS
*450 g/1 lb/2⅓ cups basmati rice
75 g/3 oz/6 tbsp unsalted butter
1 tbsp corn oil
1 bay leaf
6 black peppercorns
4 green cardamom pods
1 tsp salt
75 g/3 oz/½ cup sultanas (golden raisins)
50 g/2 oz/½ cup flaked (slivered) almonds
1 litre/1¾ pints/4 cups water*

1 Wash the rice twice, drain and set
aside in a sieve (strainer).

2 ▲ Heat the butter and oil in a
medium saucepan. Lower the heat and
throw in the bay leaf, peppercorns and
cardamoms, and fry for about 30
seconds.

3 ▲ Add the rice, salt, sultanas (golden
raisins) and flaked (slivered) almonds.
Stir-fry for about 1 minute, then pour
in the water. Bring to the boil, then
cover with a tightly-fitting lid and lower
the heat. Cook for 15–20 minutes.

4 Turn off the heat and leave the rice
to stand, still covered, for about 5
minutes before serving.

*Colourful Pullao Rice (top) and Fruity
Pullao*

Tomato Rice

This is delicious and can be eaten as a complete meal on its own.

SERVES 4

INGREDIENTS
2 tbsp corn oil
1/2 tsp onion seeds
1 medium onion, sliced
2 medium tomatoes, sliced
1 orange or yellow (bell) pepper, sliced
1 tsp ginger pulp
1 tsp garlic pulp
1 tsp chilli powder
2 tbsp chopped fresh coriander (cilantro)
1 medium potato, diced
1 1/2 tsp salt
50 g/2 oz/1/3 cup frozen peas
400 g/14 oz/2 cups basmati rice, washed
700 ml/24 fl oz/3 cups water

NUTRITIONAL VALUES (per portion)	
Total fat	6.48 g
Saturated fat	0.86 g
Cholesterol	0.00 mg
Energy (kcals/kj)	351/1475

1 ▲ Heat the oil and fry the onion seeds for about 30 seconds. Add the sliced onion and fry for about 5 minutes.

2 ▲ Start adding the sliced tomatoes, (bell) pepper, ginger, garlic, chilli powder, fresh coriander (cilantro), potatoes, salt and peas and stir-fry over a medium heat for a further 5 minutes.

3 Add the rice and stir for about 1 minute.

4 Pour in the water and bring to the boil, then lower the heat to medium. Cover and cook for 12–15 minutes. Leave the rice to stand for 5 minutes and then serve.

Pea and Mushroom Pullao

It is best to use button mushrooms and petit pois for this delectable rice dish as they make the pullao look truly attractive and appetizing.

SERVES 6

INGREDIENTS
2 tbsp vegetable oil
1/2 tsp black cumin seeds
2 black cardamom pods
2 cinnamon sticks
3 garlic cloves, sliced
1 tsp salt
1 medium tomato, sliced
50 g/2 oz/2/3 cup button mushrooms
450 g/1 lb/2 1/4 cups basmati rice
75 g/3 oz/heaped 1/3 cup petit pois
750 ml/1 1/4 pints/good 3 cups water

NUTRITIONAL VALUES (per portion)	
Total fat	4.34 g
Saturated fat	0.49 g
Cholesterol	0.00 mg
Energy (kcals/kj)	297/1246

1 Wash the rice at least twice and set aside in a sieve (strainer).

2 ▲ In a medium saucepan, heat the oil and add the spices, garlic and salt.

3 ▲ Add the sliced tomato and button mushrooms and stir-fry for 2–3 minutes.

4 Now add the rice and peas and gently stir around, making sure you do not break the rice.

5 Add the water and bring the mixture to the boil. Lower the heat, cover and continue to cook for 15–20 minutes.

Tomato Rice (top) and Pea and Mushroom Pullao

Rice Layered with Chicken and Potatoes

This dish, Murgh Biryani, is mainly prepared for important occasions, and is truly fit for royalty. Every cook in India has a subtle variation which is kept a closely guarded secret.

SERVES 4–6

INGREDIENTS
1.5 kg/3 lb chicken breast fillet, skinned and cut into large pieces
4 tbsp biryani masala paste
2 fresh green chillies, chopped
1 tbsp ginger pulp
1 tbsp garlic pulp
50 g/2 oz/2 cups fresh coriander (cilantro), chopped
6–8 fresh mint leaves, chopped, or 1 tsp mint sauce
150 ml/1/4 pint/2/3 cup natural (plain) yogurt, beaten
2 tbsp tomato purée (paste)
4 onions, finely sliced, deep-fried and crushed
salt, to taste
450 g/1 lb/2 1/4 cups basmati rice, washed and drained
1 tsp black cumin seeds
1 piece cinnamon stick, 5 cm/2 in long
4 green cardamom pods
2 black cardamom pods
vegetable oil, for shallow-frying
4 large potatoes, peeled and quartered
175 ml/6 fl oz/3/4 cup milk, mixed with 6 tbsp water
1 sachet saffron powder, mixed with 6 tbsp milk
2 tbsp ghee or unsalted (sweet) butter

Garnish
ghee or unsalted (sweet) butter, for shallow-frying
50 g/2 oz/1/3 cup cashew nuts
50 g/2 oz/1/3 cup sultanas (golden raisins)

1 ▲ Mix the chicken pieces with the next 10 ingredients in a large bowl and allow to marinate in a cool place for about 2 hours. Place in a large heavy pan and cook over a low heat for about 10 minutes. Set aside.

2 ▲ Boil a large pan of water and soak the rice with the cumin seeds, cinnamon stick and green and black cardamom pods for about 5 minutes. Drain well. If you prefer, some of the whole spices may be removed at this stage and discarded.

3 ▲ Heat the oil for shallow-frying and fry the potatoes until they are evenly browned on all sides. Drain the potatoes and set aside.

4 ▲ Place half the rice on top of the chicken in the pan in an even layer. Then make an even layer with the potatoes. Put the remaining rice on top of the potatoes and spread to make an even layer.

5 ▲ Sprinkle the water mixed with milk all over the rice. Make random holes through the rice with the handle of a spoon and pour into each a little saffron milk. Place a few knobs of ghee or butter on the surface, cover and cook over a low heat for 35–45 minutes.

6 ▲ While the biryani is cooking, make the garnish. Heat a little ghee or butter and fry the cashew nuts and sultanas (golden raisins) until they swell. Drain and set aside. When the biryani is ready, gently toss the rice, chicken and potatoes together, garnish with the nut mixture and serve hot.

Chicken Pullao

This dish is a complete meal on its own, but is also delicious served with a lentil dish such as Tarka Dhal.

SERVES 4

INGREDIENTS

75 g/3 oz/6 tbsp low-fat margarine
1 medium onion, sliced
1/4 tsp mixed onion and mustard seeds
3 curry leaves
1 tsp ginger pulp
1 tsp garlic pulp
1 tsp ground coriander
1 tsp chilli powder
1 1/2 tsp salt
2 tomatoes, sliced
1 medium potato, cubed
50 g/2 oz/1/3 cup frozen peas
175 g/6 oz/1 1/4 cups chicken, skinned, boned and cubed
400 g/14 oz/2 cups basmati rice
4 tbsp chopped fresh coriander (cilantro)
2 fresh green chillies, chopped
700 ml/24 fl oz/3 cups water

NUTRITIONAL VALUES (per portion)	
Total fat	8.50 g
Saturated fat	1.96 g
Cholesterol	25.06 mg
Energy (kcals/kj)	406/1707

1 Wash and soak the rice for 30 minutes, then set aside in a sieve (strainer).

2 ▲ In a medium saucepan, melt the low-fat margarine and fry the sliced onion until golden.

3 ▲ Add the onion and mustard seeds, the curry leaves, ginger, garlic, ground coriander, chilli powder and salt. Stir-fry for about 2 minutes.

4 ▲ Add the sliced tomatoes, cubed potato, peas and chicken and mix everything together well.

5 ▲ Add the rice and stir gently to combine with the other ingredients.

6 ▲ Finally, add the fresh coriander (cilantro) and chopped green chillies. Mix and stir-fry for a further 1 minute. Pour in the water.

7 Bring to the boil and lower the heat. Cover and cook for about 20 minutes.

Lamb Pullao

A pullao is a rice dish containing whole spices, which can either be plain or combined with meat, chicken or vegetables. Here it is made with minced (ground) lamb cooked in yogurt with a variety of spices. It makes a complete meal served on its own or served with Raita.

SERVES 4–6

INGREDIENTS
2 tbsp corn oil
1 tbsp unsalted butter or ghee
2 medium onions, sliced
1 tsp garlic pulp
1 tsp chilli powder
¼ tsp ginger pulp
¼ tsp turmeric
1 tsp garam masala
1 tsp salt
2 tbsp natural (plain) yogurt
2 medium tomatoes, sliced
450 g/1 lb lean minced (ground) lamb
2 tbsp chopped fresh coriander (cilantro)
2 medium fresh chillies, chopped
tomato slices (optional)

Rice
450 g/1 lb/2¼ cups basmati rice
1.2 litres/2 pints/5 cups water
4 cloves
4 green cardamom pods
½ tsp black cumin seeds
6 black peppercorns
1½ tsp salt
1 tbsp chopped fresh coriander
2 fresh green chillies, chopped
1 tbsp lime juice
½ tsp saffron strands soaked in 2 tbsp milk (optional)

1 Wash the rice twice, drain and set aside in a sieve (strainer).

2 Heat the oil and ghee in a deep round-bottomed frying pan (skillet) or a large karahi. Add the onions and fry until golden brown.

3 ▲ Lower the heat to medium and add the garlic, chilli powder, ginger, turmeric, garam masala, salt, yogurt and tomatoes and stir-fry gently for about 1 minute.

4 ▲ Add the minced (ground) lamb and turn up the heat to high. Use a slotted spoon to fry the lamb, scraping the bottom of the pan to prevent it from burning.

5 ▲ Add the fresh coriander (cilantro) and chillies, and continue to stir, breaking up any lumps in the meat as you work. Once the lamb is throughly cooked, set it to one side.

6 Put the rice into a large saucepan with the water, cloves, cardamoms, cumin seeds, peppercorns and salt, and bring to boil. When the rice has boiled for 2 minutes, drain off the water along with half the rice, leaving the rest in the saucepan.

7 ▲ Spread the cooked lamb over the rice in the saucepan and cover with the rice left in the strainer.

8 ▲ Add the fresh coriander, green chillies, lime juice and saffron in milk if using.

9 Cover the saucepan with a tight-fitting lid and cook over a very low heat for 15–20 minutes.

10 ▲ Check that the rice is cooked through and mix gently with a slotted spoon before serving. Garnish with slices of tomato if wished.

Rice Layered with Prawns (Shrimp)

This dish makes a meal in itself, requiring only pickles or Raita as an accompaniment. If serving for a party, complete your table with Boiled Egg Curry and Potatoes in a Red Hot Sauce.

SERVES 4–6

INGREDIENTS

2 large onions, finely sliced and deep-fried
300 ml/1/2 pint/1 1/4 cups natural (plain) yogurt
2 tbsp tomato purée (paste)
4 tbsp green masala paste
2 tbsp lemon juice
salt, to taste
1 tsp black cumin seeds
1 piece cinnamon stick, 5 cm/2 in long, or 1/4 tsp ground cinnamon
4 green cardamom pods
450 g/1 lb fresh king prawns (jumbo shrimp), peeled and deveined
225 g/8 oz/2 2/3 cups small whole button mushrooms
225 g/8 oz/1 1/3 cups frozen peas, thawed and drained
450 g/1 lb/2 1/4 cups basmati rice soaked for 5 minutes in boiled water and drained
300 ml/1/2 pint/1 1/4 cups water
1 sachet saffron powder mixed with 6 tbsp milk
2 tbsp ghee or unsalted (sweet) butter

1 ▲ Mix the first 9 ingredients together in a large bowl. Fold the prawns (shrimp), mushrooms and peas into the marinade and set aside in a cool place for about 2 hours.

2 ▲ Grease the base of a heavy pan and add the prawns, vegetables and any marinade juices. Cover with the drained rice and smooth the surface gently until you have an even layer.

3 ▲ Pour the water all over the surface of the rice. Make random holes through the rice with the handle of a spoon and pour a little saffron milk into each hole.

4 ▲ Place a few knobs of ghee or butter on the surface and place a circular piece of foil directly on top of the rice. Cover and cook over a low heat for 45–50 minutes. Gently toss the rice, prawns and vegetables together and serve hot.

Paratha

A richer, softer and flakier variation on chapatis, Parathas require a longer preparation time so plan your menu well ahead. Like chapatis, Parathas can be kept warm wrapped in foil.

MAKES 12–15

INGREDIENTS
350 g/12 oz/2¼ cups chapati (ata) flour, or use wholemeal (whole-wheat) flour, plus extra for dusting
50 g/2 oz/½ cup plain (all-purpose) flour
salt, to taste
about 2 tbsp ghee, melted
water, to mix

I ▲ Sift the flours and salt into a large mixing bowl. Make a well in the centre and add 2 tsp of the ghee and rub into the flour to make a crumbly texture. Very gradually add enough water to make a soft but pliable dough. Cover and leave to rest for 1 hour.

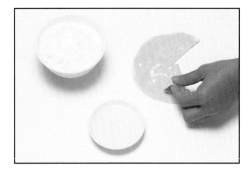

2 ▲ Divide the dough into 12–15 equal portions and keep covered. Take one portion at a time and roll out on a lightly floured surface into a circle about 10 cm/4 in in diameter. Brush with a little of the melted ghee and sprinkle with flour. With a sharp knife, make a straight cut from the centre to the edge.

3 ▲ Lift a cut edge and roll the dough into a cone shape.

4 Lift it and flatten it again into a ball. Roll the dough again on a floured surface into a circle about 17.5 cm/7 in in diameter.

5 ▲ Heat a griddle and cook one paratha at a time, placing a little of the remaining ghee along the edges. Cook the parathas on each side until golden brown. Serve hot.

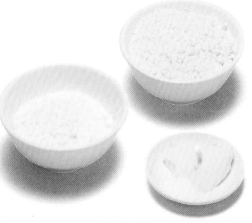

Wholemeal (Whole-Wheat) Chapatis

Chapatis are prepared daily in most Indian homes. They are best eaten as soon as they are cooked although they can be kept warm, wrapped in foil and placed in a warm oven.

MAKES 10–12

INGREDIENTS
*350 g/12 oz/2¼ cups chapati (ata) flour, or use wholemeal (whole-wheat) flour, plus extra for dusting
1 tsp salt
water, to mix
few drops of vegetable oil, for brushing
ghee or unsalted (sweet) butter, for spreading*

1 ▲ Sift the flour and salt into a large bowl. Make a well in the centre and slowly add small quantities of water until you have a smooth but pliable dough. Grease the palms of your hands and knead the dough well. Keep covered until you are ready to use.

2 Divide the dough into 10–12 equal portions, using one portion at a time and keeping the rest covered. Knead each portion into a ball.

3 Flatten the ball with your hands and place on a floured surface. Roll out until you have a circle about 17.5 cm/ 7 in in diameter.

4 ▲ Heat a heavy griddle and, when hot, roast the chapatis on each side, pressing the edges down gently. When both sides are ready, brush the first side lightly with ghee or butter.

Naan

Traditionally, Naans are baked in a tandoor or clay oven, although these naans cooked in a conventional oven look just as authentic.

MAKES 6–8

INGREDIENTS
*2 tsp dried (active dry) yeast
4 tbsp warm milk
2 tsp sugar
450 g/1 lb/4 cups plain (all-purpose) flour
1 tsp baking powder
½ tsp salt
150 ml/¼ pint/⅔ cup milk
150 ml/¼ pint/⅔ cup natural (plain) yogurt, beaten
1 egg, beaten
2 tbsp ghee, melted
flour, for dusting
ghee, for greasing
chopped fresh coriander (cilantro) and onion seeds, to sprinkle*

1 ▲ Mix the yeast, warm milk and sugar and leave to become frothy. Sift together the flour, baking powder and salt. Make a well in the centre and add the yeast mixture, milk, yogurt, egg and ghee. Fold in all the ingredients.

2 Knead the dough well. Tightly cover the bowl and keep in a warm place until the dough doubles in size. To test, push a finger into the dough – it should spring back. Preheat the oven to 200°C/400°F/Gas 6. Roll out the dough on a floured surface.

3 ▲ Make each naan slipper-shaped, about 25 cm/10 in long and about 15 cm/6 in wide, tapering to 5 cm/2 in. Sprinkle with the coriander and onion seeds, Place on greased trays and bake in the preheated oven for 10–12 minutes.

Wholemeal (Whole-Wheat) Chapatis (top) and Naan

Side Dishes

Part of the charm of eating an Indian meal is the rich assortment of taste sensations. Cool and tangy Spiced Yogurt or Raita make a refreshing contrast to a fiery curry, while Mango Chutney and Fresh Coriander Relish add a piquant touch. Salads are often served as side dishes and a simple Tomato Salad or Avocado Salad are perfect to serve with many curried foods.

Sweet Potato and Carrot Salad

`LOW-FAT RECIPE`

This salad has a sweet-and-sour taste, and can be served warm as part of a meal or eaten in a larger quantity as a main course.

SERVES 4

INGREDIENTS
1 medium sweet potato
2 carrots, cut into thick diagonal slices
3 medium tomatoes
8–10 iceberg lettuce leaves
75 g/3 oz/½ cup canned chick-peas
*   (garbanzos), drained*

Dressing
1 tbsp clear honey
6 tbsp natural (plain) low-fat yogurt
½ tsp salt
1 tsp coarsely ground black pepper

Garnish
1 tbsp walnuts
1 tbsp sultanas (golden raisins)
1 small onion, cut into rings

NUTRITIONAL VALUES (per portion)	
Total fat	4.85 g
Saturated fat	0.58 g
Cholesterol	0.85 mg
Energy (kcals/kj)	176/741

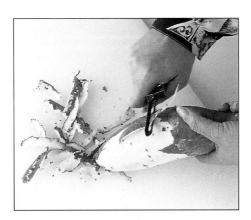

1 ▲ Peel the sweet potato and roughly dice. Boil until soft but not mushy, cover the pan and set aside.

2 Boil the carrots for a just a few minutes making sure they remain crunchy. Add the carrots to the sweet potatoes.

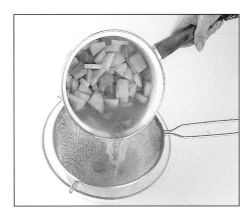

3 ▲ Drain the water from the sweet potatoes and carrots and place together in a bowl.

4 ▲ Slice the tops off the tomatoes, then scoop out and discard the seeds. Roughly chop the flesh.

5 ▲ Line a glass bowl with the lettuce leaves. Mix together the sweet potatoes, carrots, chick-peas (garbanzos) and tomatoes and place in the bowl.

6 ▲ Blend together all the dressing ingredients and beat using a fork.

7 ▲ Garnish with the walnuts, sultanas (golden raisins) and onion rings. Pour the dressing over the salad or serve it in a separate bowl, if wished.

Spiced Yogurt

Yogurt is always a welcome accompaniment to hot curries. This has been given a final fry with spices just to flavour the yogurt slightly.

MAKES 450 ML/¾ PINT/SCANT 2 CUPS

INGREDIENTS
450 ml/¾ pint/scant 2 cups plain yogurt
½ tsp freshly ground fennel seeds
salt, to taste
½ tsp sugar
4 tbsp vegetable oil
1 dried red chilli
¼ tsp mustard seeds
¼ tsp cumin seeds
4–6 curry leaves
pinch each, asafoetida and turmeric

1 ▲ In a heatproof serving dish, mix together the yogurt, fennel, salt and sugar and chill until you are nearly ready to serve.

2 ▲ Heat the oil in a frying pan (skillet) and fry the chilli, mustard and cumin seeds, curry leaves, asafoetida and turmeric. When the chilli turns dark, pour the oil and spices over the yogurt. Fold the yogurt together with the spices at the table before serving.

Raita

Raitas are served to cool the effect of hot curries. Cucumber and mint raita is most commonly served, so why not try a variation?

SERVES 4

INGREDIENTS
350 ml/12 fl oz/1¹/₂ cups natural (plain) yogurt
75 g/3 oz seedless grapes
50 g/2 oz shelled walnuts
2 firm bananas
1 tsp sugar
salt, to taste
1 tsp freshly ground cumin seeds
¹/₄ tsp freshly roasted cumin seeds, chilli powder or paprika, to garnish

1 ▲ Place the yogurt in a chilled bowl and add the grapes and walnuts. Slice the bananas directly into the bowl and fold in gently before the bananas turn brown.

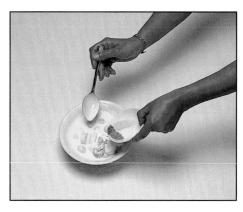

2 ▲ Add the sugar, salt and ground cumin, and gently mix together. Chill, and just before serving, sprinkle on the cumin seeds, chilli powder or paprika.

Spinach and Mushroom Salad

This salad is especially good served with the Glazed Garlic Prawns (Shrimp).

SERVES 4

INGREDIENTS
20 small spinach leaves
10 baby corn cobs
25 g/1 oz salad (garden) cress (optional)
115 g/4 oz/1½ cups mushrooms
8–10 onion rings
2 medium tomatoes
salt
crushed black peppercorns
2 fresh coriander (cilantro) sprigs
(optional)
3–4 lime slices (optional)

NUTRITIONAL VALUES (per portion)	
Total fat	0.93 g
Saturated fat	0.12 g
Cholesterol	0.00 mg
Energy (kcals/kj)	38/161

1 ▲ Halve the baby corn cobs, and slice the mushrooms and tomatoes.

2 ▲ Arrange all the salad ingredients in a bowl. Season with salt and pepper and garnish with fresh coriander (cilantro) and lime slices, if wished.

Nutty Salad

A delicious and filling salad which can be served as an accompaniment or as an appetizer.

SERVES 4

INGREDIENTS
1 medium onion, cut into 12 rings
115 g/4 oz/½ cup canned red kidney
beans, drained
1 medium green courgette (zucchini),
sliced
1 medium yellow courgette, sliced
50 g/2 oz/²⁄₃ cup pasta shells, cooked
50 g/2 oz/½ cup cashew nuts
25 g/1 oz/¼ cup peanuts

Dressing
120 ml/4 fl oz/½ cup fromage frais
2 tbsp natural (plain) low-fat yogurt
1 fresh green chilli, chopped
1 tbsp chopped fresh coriander (cilantro)
½ tsp salt
½ tsp crushed black peppercorns

½ tsp crushed dried red chillies
1 tbsp lemon juice
lime wedges

NUTRITIONAL VALUES (per portion)	
Total fat	7.14 g
Saturated fat	1.09 g
Cholesterol	0.56 mg
Energy (kcals/kj)	153/642

1 Arrange the onion rings, red kidney beans, courgette (zucchini) slices and pasta in a salad dish and sprinkle the cashew nuts and peanuts over the top.

2 ▲ In a separate bowl, blend together the fromage frais, yogurt, green chilli, fresh coriander (cilantro) and salt and beat it well using a fork.

3 Sprinkle the black pepper, crushed red chillies and lemon juice over the dressing. Garnish the salad with the lime wedges and serve with the dressing in a separate bowl or poured over the salad.

Spinach and Mushroom Salad (top) and Nutty Salad

Tomato Salad

This is a simple relish served with most meals. It provides a contrast to hot curries, with its crunchy texture and refreshing ingredients.

SERVES 4–6

INGREDIENTS
2 limes
1/2 tsp sugar
salt and freshly ground black pepper, to taste
2 onions, finely chopped
4 firm tomatoes, finely chopped
1/2 cucumber, finely chopped
1 green chilli, finely chopped
few fresh coriander (cilantro) leaves, chopped
few fresh mint leaves, to garnish

1 ▲ Squeeze the juice of the limes into a glass bowl and add the sugar, salt and pepper. Allow to rest until the sugar and salt have dissolved, stirring occasionally. Mix together well.

2 ▲ Add the onions, tomatoes, cucumber, chilli and fresh coriander (cilantro) leaves. Chill, and garnish with mint before serving.

Fresh Coriander (Cilantro) Relish

Delicious as an accompaniment to kebabs, samosas and bhajias, this relish can also be used as a spread for cucumber or tomato sandwiches.

MAKES 400 G/14 OZ/1¾ CUPS

INGREDIENTS

2 tbsp vegetable oil

1 dried red chilli

¼ tsp each, cumin, fennel and onion seeds

¼ tsp asafoetida

4 curry leaves

115 g/4 oz/2 cups desiccated (shredded) coconut

2 tsp sugar

salt, to taste

3 fresh green chillies

175 g–225 g/6–8 oz fresh coriander (cilantro)

4 tbsp mint sauce

juice of 3 lemons

1 ▲ Heat the oil in a frying pan (skillet). Fry the dried chilli, the cumin, fennel and onion seeds, the asafoetida, curry leaves, desiccated (shredded) coconut, sugar and salt until the coconut turns golden brown. Cool.

2 ▲ Grind the spice mixture with the green chillies, fresh coriander (cilantro) and mint sauce. Moisten with lemon juice. Remove, and chill before serving.

Yogurt Salad

A delicious salad with a yogurt base, this is really an Eastern version of coleslaw.

SERVES 4

INGREDIENTS
350 ml/12 fl oz/1½ cups natural (plain) low-fat yogurt
2 tsp clear honey
2 medium carrots, thickly sliced
2 spring onions (scallions), roughly chopped
115 g/4 oz/1½ cups cabbage, finely shredded
50 g/2 oz/⅓ cup sultanas (golden raisins)
50 g/2 oz/½ cup cashew nuts
16 white grapes, halved
½ tsp salt
1 tsp chopped fresh mint
3–4 mint sprigs (optional)

NUTRITIONAL VALUES (per portion)	
Total fat	7.62 g
Saturated fat	1.20 g
Cholesterol	3.40 mg
Energy (kcals/kj)	201/846

1 ▲ Using a fork, beat the yogurt in a bowl with the clear honey.

2 Mix together the carrots, spring onions (scallions), cabbage, sultanas (golden raisins), cashew nuts, grapes, salt and chopped mint.

3 ▲ Pour the yogurt mixture over the salad and blend everything together.

4 Transfer to a serving dish and garnish with the mint sprigs, if wished.

Spicy Baby Vegetable Salad

This warm vegetable salad makes an excellent accompaniment to almost any main course dish.

SERVES 6

INGREDIENTS
10 baby potatoes, halved
15 baby carrots
10 baby courgettes (zucchini)
115 g/4 oz/1½ cups button mushrooms

Dressing
3 tbsp lemon juice
1½ tbsp olive oil
1 tbsp chopped fresh coriander (cilantro)
1 tsp salt
2 small fresh green chillies, finely chopped

NUTRITIONAL VALUES (per portion)	
Total fat	3.54 g
Saturated fat	0.48 g
Cholesterol	0.00 mg
Energy (kcals/kj)	76/319

1 Wash and boil all the baby vegetables until tender. Drain and place these in a serving dish.

2 ▲ In a separate bowl, mix together all the ingredients for the dressing.

3 Toss the vegetables in the dressing and serve.

Yogurt Salad (top) and Spicy Baby Vegetable Salad

Avocado Salad

In India, avocados are called butter fruit, reflecting their subtle taste. This delicate dish makes a good appetizer.

SERVES 4

INGREDIENTS
2 avocados
5 tbsp natural (plain) yogurt, beaten
115 g/4 oz/¹/₂ cup cottage cheese with chives
1 clove garlic, crushed
2 fresh green chillies, finely chopped
salt and pepper, to taste
lemon juice
mixed salad leaves, shredded
paprika and fresh mint leaves, to garnish

1 ▲ Halve the avocados and remove the stones (pits). Gently scoop out the flesh, reserving the skins, and cut into small cubes. In a bowl, mix the yogurt, cottage cheese, garlic, chillies and salt and pepper and fold in the avocado cubes. Chill in the refrigerator.

2 ▲ Rub the avocado skins with some lemon juice and line each cavity with some shredded salad leaves. Top with the chilled mixture, garnish with the paprika and mint leaves and serve immediately.

Indian Fruit Salad

This is a very appetizing and refreshing salad, with a typically Indian combination of citrus fruits seasoned with salt and pepper. It will provide the perfect ending to a heavy meal.

SERVES 6

INGREDIENTS
115 g/4 oz seedless green and black grapes
225 g/8 oz canned mandarin segments, drained
2 navel oranges, peeled and segmented
225 g/8 oz canned grapefruit segments, drained
1 honeydew melon cut into balls
¹/₂ watermelon cut into balls
1 fresh mango, peeled and sliced
juice of 1 lemon

salt and freshly ground black pepper, to taste
¹/₂ tsp sugar
¹/₄ tsp freshly ground cumin seeds

1 ▲ Place all the fruit in a large serving bowl and add the lemon juice. Toss gently to prevent damaging the fruit.

2 ▲ Mix together the remaining ingredients and sprinkle over the fruit. Gently toss, chill thoroughly and serve.

Avocado Salad (top) and Indian Fruit Salad

Tomato Chutney

This delicious relish is especially suited to lentil dishes. If kept refrigerated, it can be made a week before serving.

MAKES 450–500 G/16–18 OZ/2–2¼ CUPS

INGREDIENTS
6 tbsp vegetable oil
1 piece cinnamon stick, 5 cm/2 in long
4 cloves
1 tsp freshly roasted cumin seeds
1 tsp nigella seeds
4 bay leaves
1 tsp mustard seeds, crushed
4 cloves garlic, crushed
1 piece fresh ginger, 5 cm/2 in long, crushed
1 tsp chilli powder
1 tsp turmeric
4 tbsp brown sugar

800 g/1¾ lb canned, chopped tomatoes, drained (reserving juices)

1 ▲ Heat the oil over a medium heat and fry the cinnamon, cloves, cumin and nigella seeds, bay leaves and mustard seeds for about 5 minutes. Add the garlic and fry until golden.

2 ▲ Add the ginger, chilli powder, turmeric, sugar and the reserved tomato juices. Simmer until reduced, add the tomatoes and cook for 15–20 minutes. Cool and serve.

Mango Chutney

Chutneys are usually served as an accompaniment to curry but this one is particularly nice served in a cheese sandwich or as a dip with papadums.

MAKES 450 G/I LB/2 CUPS

INGREDIENTS
4 tbsp malt vinegar
1/2 tsp crushed dried chillies
6 cloves
6 peppercorns
1 tsp roasted cumin seeds
1/2 tsp onion seeds
salt, to taste
175 g/6 oz/3/4 cup sugar
450 g/1 lb green (unripe) mango, peeled and cubed
1 piece fresh ginger, 5 cm/2 in long, finely sliced
2 cloves garlic, crushed
thin peel of 1 orange or lemon (optional)

1 ▲ In a saucepan, heat the vinegar with the chillies, cloves, peppercorns, cumin and onion seeds, salt and sugar. Simmer until the flavours of the spices infuse into the vinegar – about 15 minutes on a low heat.

2 ▲ Add the mango, ginger, garlic and peel, if using. Simmer until the mango is mushy and most of the vinegar has evaporated. When cool, pour into sterilized bottles. Leave for a few days before serving.

Hot Lime Pickle

A good lime pickle is not only delicious served with any meal, but it increases the appetite and aids digestion.

MAKES 450 G/I LB/2 CUPS

INGREDIENTS
25 limes
225 g/8 oz salt
50 g/2 oz fenugreek powder
50 g/2 oz mustard powder
150 g/5 oz chilli powder
15 g/¹/₂ oz turmeric
600 ml/1pint/2¹/₂ cups mustard oil
1 tsp asafoetida
25 g/1 oz yellow mustard seeds, crushed

1 ▲ Cut each lime into 8 pieces and remove the pips, if you wish. Place the limes in a large sterilized jar or glass bowl. Add the salt and toss with the limes. Cover and leave in a warm place for 1–2 weeks, until they become soft and dull brown in colour.

2 Mix together the fenugreek, mustard powder, chilli powder and turmeric and add to the limes.

3 Cover and leave to rest in a warm place for a further 2 or 3 days.

4 ▲ Heat the mustard oil in a frying pan and fry the asafoetida and mustard seeds. When the oil reaches smoking point, pour it over the limes. Mix well, cover with a clean cloth and leave in a warm place for about 1 week before serving.

Green Chilli Pickle

Southern India is the source of some of the hottest curries and pickles, which are said to cool the body.

MAKES 450–550 G/I–I¹/₄ LB/2–2¹/₂ CUPS

INGREDIENTS
50 g/2 oz yellow mustard seeds, crushed
50 g/2 oz freshly ground cumin seeds
25 g/1 oz turmeric
50 g/2 oz garlic cloves, crushed
150 ml/¹/₄ pint/²/₃ cup white vinegar
75 g/3 oz/¹/₃ cup sugar
2 tsp salt
150 ml/¹/₄ pint/²/₃ cup mustard oil
20 small garlic cloves
450 g/1 lb small fresh green chillies, halved

1 ▲ Mix the mustard and cumin seeds, the turmeric, crushed garlic, vinegar, sugar and salt together in a sterilized glass bowl. Cover with a cloth and allow to rest for 24 hours. This enables the spices to infuse and the sugar and salt to melt.

2 Heat the mustard oil in a frying pan (skillet) and gently fry the spice mixture for about 5 minutes. (Keep a window open while cooking with mustard oil as it is pungent and the smoke may irritate the eyes.) Add the garlic cloves and fry for a further 5 minutes.

3 ▲ Add the chillies and cook gently until tender but still green in colour. This will take about 30 minutes on a low heat. Cool thoroughly and pour into sterilized bottles, ensuring the oil is evenly distributed if you are using more than one bottle. Leave to rest for a week before serving.

Hot Lime Pickle (top) and Green Chilli Pickle

Apricot Chutney

Chutneys can add zest to most meals, and in Pakistan you will usually find a selection of different kinds served in tiny bowls for people to choose from. Dried apricots are readily available from supermarkets or health food shops.

MAKES ABOUT 450 g/1 lb

INGREDIENTS
450 g/1 lb/3 cups dried apricots, finely diced
1 tsp garam masala
275 g/10 oz/1¼ cups soft light brown sugar
450 ml/¾ pint/scant 2 cups malt vinegar
1 tsp ginger pulp
1 tsp salt
75 g/3 oz/½ cup sultanas (golden raisins)
450 ml/¾ pint/scant 2 cups water

1 ▲ Put all the ingredients into a medium saucepan and mix together thoroughly.

2 ▲ Bring to the boil, then turn down the heat and simmer for 30–35 minutes, stirring occasionally.

3 When the chutney has thickened to a fairly stiff consistency, transfer into 2–3 clean jam jars and leave to cool. This chutney should be stored in the refrigerator.

Tasty Toasts

These crunchy toasts make an ideal snack or part of a brunch. They are especially delicious served with grilled (broiled) tomatoes and baked beans.

MAKES 4

INGREDIENTS
4 eggs
300 ml/½ pint/1¼ cups milk
2 fresh green chillies, finely chopped
2 tbsp chopped fresh coriander (cilantro)
75 g/3 oz/¾ cup Cheddar or mozzarella cheese, grated
½ tsp salt
¼ tsp freshly ground black pepper
4 slices bread
corn oil for frying

1 Break the eggs into a medium bowl and whisk together. Slowly add the milk and whisk again. Add the chillies, coriander (cilantro), cheese, salt and pepper.

2 Cut the bread slices in half diagonally, and soak them, one at a time, in the egg mixture.

3 ▼ Heat the oil in a medium frying pan (skillet) and fry the bread slices over a medium heat, turning them once or twice, until they are golden brown.

4 Drain off any excess oil as you remove the toasts from the pan and serve immediately.

Apricot Chutney (top) and Tasty Toasts

Desserts & Drinks

After a hot, spicy meal, Mango Sorbet with Sauce is a welcome, light dessert, while Light Vermicelli Pudding — delicately flavoured with saffron and tossed with coconut, almonds and pistachios — is ideal after a less substantial main course. On a hot day, or with hot food, there is no substitute for Sweet Lassi, a refreshing and delicious chilled yogurt drink.

Rich Rice Pudding

*B*oth Muslim and Hindu communities prepare Kheer, which is traditionally served at mosques and temples.

SERVES 4–6

INGREDIENTS
1 tbsp ghee
1 piece cinnamon stick, 5 cm/2 in long
175 g/6 oz/³⁄4 cup soft brown sugar
115 g/4 oz/1 cup coarsely ground rice
1.2 litres/2 pints/5 cups full cream (whole) milk
1 tsp ground cardamom
50 g/2 oz/¹⁄3 cup sultanas (golden raisins)
25 g/1 oz/¹⁄4 cup flaked (slivered) almonds
¹⁄2 tsp freshly ground nutmeg, to serve

1 ▲ In a heavy pan, melt the ghee and fry the cinnamon and sugar. Keep frying until the sugar begins to caramelize. Reduce the heat immediately when this happens.

2 Add the rice and half the milk. Bring to the boil, stirring constantly to avoid the milk boiling over. Reduce the heat and simmer until the rice is cooked, stirring regularly.

3 ▲ Add the remaining milk, cardamom, sultanas (golden raisins) and almonds and leave to simmer, but keep stirring to prevent the kheer from sticking to the base of the pan. When the mixture has thickened, serve hot or cold, sprinkled with the nutmeg.

Classic Vermicelli Pudding

*T*his sweet is prepared by Muslims very early in the morning of Id-ul-Fitr, the feast after the 30 days of Ramadan.

SERVES 4–6

INGREDIENTS
6 tbsp ghee
115 g/4 oz/1 cup vermicelli, coarsely broken
25 g/1 oz/¹⁄4 cup flaked (slivered) almonds
25 g/1 oz/¹⁄4 cup pistachios, slivered
25 g/1 oz cudapah nuts
50 g/2 oz/¹⁄3 cup sultanas (golden raisins)
50 g/2 oz dates, stoned (pitted) and slivered
1.2 litres/2 pints/5 cups full cream (whole) milk
4 tbsp dark brown sugar
1 sachet saffron powder

1 ▲ Heat 4 tbsp of the ghee in a frying pan (skillet) and sauté the vermicelli until golden brown. (If you are using the Italian variety, sauté it a little longer.) Remove and set aside.

2 Heat the remaining ghee and fry the nuts, sultanas (golden raisins) and dates until the sultanas swell. Add to the vermicelli.

3 ▲ Heat the milk in a large heavy pan and add the sugar. Bring to the boil, add the vermicelli mixture and boil, stirring constantly. Reduce the heat and simmer until the vermicelli is soft and you have a fairly thick pudding. Fold in the saffron powder and serve hot or cold.

Rich Rice Pudding (top) and Classic Vermicelli Pudding

Melon and Strawberry Salad

A beautiful and colourful fruit salad, this is suitable to serve as a refreshing appetizer or to round off a meal.

SERVES 4

INGREDIENTS
1 galia melon
1 honeydew melon
½ watermelon
225 g/8 oz fresh strawberries
1 tbsp lemon juice
1 tbsp clear honey
1 tbsp chopped fresh mint
1 mint sprig (optional)

NUTRITIONAL VALUES (per portion)	
Total fat	0.84 g
Saturated fat	0.00 g
Cholesterol	0.00 mg
Energy (kcals/kj)	139/584

1 ▲ Prepare the melons by cutting them in half and discarding the seeds. Use a melon baller to scoop out the flesh into balls or a knife to cut it into cubes. Place these in a fruit bowl.

2 Rinse and take the stems off the strawberries, cut these in half and add them to the fruit bowl.

3 ▲ Mix together the lemon juice and clear honey and add about 1 tbsp of water to make this easier to pour over the fruit. Mix into the fruit gently.

4 ▲ Sprinkle the chopped mint over the top of the fruit. Serve garnished with the mint sprig, if wished.

COOK'S TIP

Use whichever melons are available: replace galia with cantaloupe or watermelon with charentais, for example. Try to choose three melons with a variation in colour for an attractive effect.

Caramel with Fresh Fruit

A creamy caramel dessert is a wonderful way to end a meal. It is light and delicious, and this recipe is very simple.

SERVES 6

INGREDIENTS
Caramel
2 tbsp sugar
2 tbsp water

Custard
6 medium eggs
4 drops vanilla essence (extract)
8–10 tbsp sugar
750 ml/1¼ pints/good 3 cups semi-skimmed (2%) milk
fresh fruit for serving

NUTRITIONAL VALUES (per portion)	
Total fat	7.40 g
Saturated fat	2.77 g
Cholesterol	201.25 mg
Energy (kcals/kj)	229/964

1 To make the caramel, place the sugar and water in a heatproof dish and place in a microwave and cook for 4 minutes on high or until the sugar has caramelized. Or melt in a pan until pale gold in colour. Pour into a 1.2 litre/2 pint/5 cup soufflé dish. Leave to cool.

2 ▲ Preheat the oven to 180°C/350°F/Gas 4. To make the custard, break the eggs into a medium mixing bowl and whisk until frothy.

3 ▲ Stir in the vanilla essence (extract) and gradually add the sugar then the milk, whisking continuously.

4 ▲ Pour the custard over the top of the caramel.

5 Cook in the preheated oven for 35–40 minutes. Remove from the oven and leave to cool for about 30 minutes or until set.

6 Loosen the custard from the sides of the dish with a knife. Place a serving dish upside-down on top of the soufflé dish and invert, giving a gentle shake.

7 Arrange any fruit of your choice around the caramel and serve. Strawberries, blueberries, orange rings, banana slices and raspberries form the colourful array shown here.

Indian Ice Cream

Kulfi-wallahs (ice cream vendors) have always made kulfi, and continue to this day, without using modern freezers. Kulfi is packed into metal cones sealed with dough and then churned in clay pots until set. Try this method – it works extremely well in an ordinary freezer.

SERVES 4–6

INGREDIENTS

3 × 400 ml/14 fl oz cans evaporated milk
3 egg whites, whisked until peaks form
350 g/12 oz/3 cups icing (confectioners') sugar
1 tsp ground cardamom
1 tbsp rose water
175 g/6 oz/1½ cups pistachios, chopped
75 g/3 oz/½ cup sultanas (golden raisins)
75 g/3 oz/¾ cup flaked (slivered) almonds
25 g/1 oz/3 tbsp glacé (candied) cherries, halved

1 ▲ Remove the labels from the cans of evaporated milk and lay the cans down into a pan with a tight-fitting cover. Fill the pan with water to reach three-quarters up the cans. Bring to the boil, cover and simmer for 20 minutes. When cool, remove and chill the cans in the refrigerator for 24 hours.

2 ▲ Open the cans and empty the milk into a large, chilled bowl. Whisk until it doubles in quantity, then fold in the whisked egg whites and icing (confectioners') sugar.

3 ▲ Gently fold in the remaining ingredients, seal the bowl with cling film (plastic wrap) and leave in the freezer for 1 hour.

4 ▲ Remove the ice cream from the freezer and mix well with a fork. Transfer to a serving container and return to the freezer for a final setting. Remove from the freezer 10 minutes before serving.

Mango Sorbet (Sherbet) with Sauce

After a heavy meal, this makes a very refreshing dessert. Mango is said to be one of the oldest fruits cultivated in India, having been brought by Lord Shiva for his beautiful wife, Parvathi.

SERVES 4–6

INGREDIENTS

900 g/2 lb mango pulp
½ tsp lemon juice
grated rind of 1 orange and 1 lemon
4 egg whites, whisked until peaks form
50 g/2 oz/¼ cup caster (superfine) sugar
120 ml/4 fl oz/½ cup double (heavy) cream
50 g/2 oz/½ cup icing (confectioners') sugar

3 ▲ Remove and beat again. Transfer to an ice cream container, and freeze until fully set.

4 ▲ Whip the double (heavy) cream with the icing (confectioners') sugar and the remaining mango pulp. Chill the sauce for 24 hours. Remove the sorbet (sherbet) 10 minutes before serving. Scoop out individual servings and cover with a generous helping of mango sauce. Serve immediately.

1 ▲ In a large, chilled bowl, mix half of the mango pulp, with the lemon juice and the grated rind.

2 ▲ Gently fold in the egg whites and caster (superfine) sugar. Cover with cling film (plastic wrap) and place in the freezer for at least 1 hour.

Ground Rice Pudding

This delicious and light ground rice pudding is the perfect end to a spicy meal. It can be served hot or cold.

SERVES 4–6

INGREDIENTS
50 g/2 oz/½ cup coarsely ground rice
25 g/1 oz/2 tbsp ground almonds
4 green cardamom pods, crushed
900 ml/1½ pints/3¾ cups semi-skimmed (2%) milk
6 tbsp sugar
1 tbsp rose water

Garnish
1 tbsp crushed pistachio nuts
silver leaf (varq) (optional)

NUTRITIONAL VALUES (per portion)	
Total fat	8.78 g
Saturated fat	2.57 g
Cholesterol	14.70 mg
Energy (kcals/kj)	201/844

1 ▲ Place the ground rice and almonds in a saucepan with the green cardamoms. Add 600 ml/1 pint/2½ cups milk and bring to the boil over a medium heat, stirring occasionally.

2 ▲ Add the remaining milk and cook over a medium heat for about 10 minutes or until the rice mixture thickens to the consistency of a creamy chicken soup.

3 Stir in the sugar and rose water and continue to cook for a further 2 minutes. Serve garnished with pistachio nuts and silver leaf, if wished.

Vermicelli

Indian vermicelli, made from wheat, is much finer than Italian vermicelli and is readily available from Asian stores.

SERVES 4

INGREDIENTS
115 g/4 oz/1 cup vermicelli
1.2 litres/2 pints/5 cups water
½ tsp saffron strands
1 tbsp sugar
4 tbsp low-fat fromage frais (optional)

Garnish
1 tbsp shredded fresh coconut, or desiccated (shredded) coconut
1 tbsp flaked (slivered) almonds
1 tbsp chopped pistachio nuts
1 tbsp sugar

NUTRITIONAL VALUES (per portion)	
Total fat	4.61 g
Saturated fat	1.66 g
Cholesterol	0.15 mg
Energy (kcals/kj)	319/1341

1 ▲ Crush the vermicelli in your hands and place in a saucepan. Pour in the water, add the saffron and bring to the boil. Boil for about 5 minutes.

2 ▲ Stir in the sugar and continue cooking until the water has evaporated. Strain through a sieve (strainer), if necessary, to remove any excess liquid.

3 Place the vermicelli in a serving dish and garnish with the shredded coconut, almonds, pistachio nuts and sugar. Serve with fromage frais, if wished.

Ground Rice Pudding (top) and Vermicelli

Tea and Fruit Punch

This delicious punch may be served hot or cold. White wine or brandy may be added to taste.

MAKES 875 ML/1¾ PINTS/3½ CUPS

INGREDIENTS
600 ml/1 pint/2½ cups water
1 cinnamon stick
4 cloves
2½ tsp Earl Grey tea leaves
175 g/6 oz/¾ cup sugar
450 ml/¾ pint/1½ cups tropical soft drink concentrate
1 lemon, sliced
1 small orange, sliced
½ cucumber, sliced

1 ▲ Bring the water to the boil in a saucepan with the cinnamon and cloves. Remove from the heat and add the tea leaves and allow to brew for 5 minutes. Stir and strain into a large chilled bowl.

2 ▲ Add the sugar and the soft drink concentrate and allow to rest until the sugar has dissolved and the mixture cooled. Place the fruit and cucumber in a chilled punch bowl and pour over the tea mix. Chill for 24 hours before serving.

Lassi

Lassi or buttermilk is prepared by churning yogurt with water and then removing the fat. To make this refreshing drink without churning, use low-fat natural (plain) yogurt.

SERVES 4

INGREDIENTS
450 ml/¾ pint/1½ cups natural (plain) yogurt
300 ml/½ pint/1¼ cups water
1 piece fresh ginger, 2.5 cm/1 in long, finely crushed
2 green chillies, finely chopped
½ tsp ground cumin
salt and freshly ground black pepper, to taste
few fresh coriander (cilantro) leaves, chopped, to garnish

1 ▲ In a bowl, whisk the yogurt and water until well blended. The consistency should be that of full cream (whole) milk. Adjust by adding more water if necessary.

2 ▲ Add the ginger, chillies and ground cumin, season with the salt and pepper and mix well. Divide into 4 serving glasses and chill. Garnish with coriander (cilantro) before serving.

Tea and Fruit Punch (top) and Lassi

Sweet Lassi

LOW-FAT RECIPE

Lassi is a very popular drink both in India and Pakistan. It is available not only from roadside cafés but is also a great favourite in good restaurants and hotels. There is no substitute for this drink, especially on a hot day. It is ideal served with hot dishes as it helps the body to digest spicy food.

SERVES 4

INGREDIENTS
300 ml/½ pint/1¼ cups natural (plain) low-fat yogurt
1 tsp sugar, or to taste
300 ml/½ pint/1¼ cups water
2 tbsp puréed fruit (optional)
1 tbsp crushed pistachio nuts

NUTRITIONAL VALUES (per portion)

Total fat	1.91 g
Saturated fat	0.52 g
Cholesterol	2.80 mg
Energy (kcals/kj)	60/251

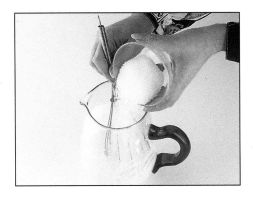

1 ▲ Place the yogurt in a jug and whisk it for about 2 minutes until frothy. Add the sugar to taste.

2 ▲ Pour in the water and the puréed fruit, if using, and continue to whisk for 2 minutes.

3 Pour the lassi into serving glasses. Serve chilled, decorated with crushed pistachio nuts.

Almond Sherbet

LOW-FAT RECIPE

Traditionally this drink was always made in the month of Ramaden, when we used to break our fast. It should be served chilled.

SERVES 4

INGREDIENTS
50 g/2 oz/½ cup ground almonds
600 ml/1 pint/2½ cups semi-skimmed (2%) milk
2 tsp sugar, or to taste

NUTRITIONAL VALUES (per portion)

Total fat	6.15 g
Saturated fat	1.70 g
Cholesterol	9.80 mg
Energy (kcals/kj)	117/492

2 ▲ Pour in the milk and sugar and stir to mix. Taste for sweetness and serve chilled.

1 ▲ Put the ground almonds into a jug.

Lassi flavoured with puréed raspberries (left) and Almond Sherbet

Stockists and Suppliers

United Kingdom

M. and S. Patel
372–382 Romford Road
London E7 8BS
(0181) 472-6201

Rafi's Spice Box
c/o 31 Schoolfield
Glemsford
Suffolk CO10 7RE
(mail order)

The Spice Shop
115–117 Drummond Street
London NW1 2HL
(0171) 387-4526

United States

Arizona

G&L Import-Export Corp.
4828 East 22nd Street
Tuscon
Arizona 85706
(602) 790-9016

Manila Oriental Foodmart
3557 West Dunlap Avenue
Phoenix
Arizona 85021
(602) 841-2977

California

Indian Food Mill
650 San Bruno Avenue East
San Bruno
California 94014
(415) 583-6559

Connecticut

India Spice & Gift Shop
3295 Fairfield Avenue
Fairfield
Connecticut 06605
(203) 384-0666

Florida

Grocery Mahat & Asian Spices
1026 South Military Trail
West Palm Beach
Florida 334436
(407) 433-3936

Illinois

Indian Groceries & Spices
7300 St Louis Avenue
Skokie
Illinois 60076
(708) 2480

Maryland

India Supermarket
8107 Fenton Street
Silver Springs
Maryland 20910
(301) 589-8423

Massachusetts

India Groceries
Oak Square
Boston
Massachusetts 02111
(617) 254-5540

New Jersey

Maharaja Indian Foods
130 Speedwell Avenue
Morristown
New Jersey 07960
(210) 829-0048

New York

Indian Groceries and Spices
61 Wythe Avenue
Brooklyn
New York 11211
(718) 963-0477

Ohio

Crestview Market
200 Crestview Road
Columbus
Ohio 43202
(614) 267-2723

Pennsylvania

Gourmail Inc.
Drawer 516
Berwyn
Pennsylvania 19312
(215) 296-4620

Texas

MGM Indian Foods
9200 Lamar Boulevard
Austin
Texas 78513
(512) 835 6937

Index